BRAD
MELTZER

WITH
KEITH FERRELL

THE 10 GREATEST
CONSPIRACIES
OF ALL TIME

WORKMAN PUBLISHING • NEW YORK

For my history teacher Ellen Sherman,
who taught me the power of asking the right questions

Library of Congress Cataloging-in-Publication Data is available.

ISBN 978-1-5235-1236-2

Workman books are available at special discounts when purchased in
bulk for premiums and sales promotions as well as for fund-raising or
educational use. Special editions or book excerpts can also be created
to specification. For details, contact the Special Sales Director at the
address following, or send an email to specialmarkets@workman.com.

Cover design by Vaughn Andrews
Book design by Lisa Hollander
Cover photo by Alamy: Alpha Historica
Originally published in 2013 as *History Decoded: The 10 Greatest
Conspiracies of All Time*

Workman Publishing Co., Inc.
225 Varick Street
New York, NY 10014-4381
workman.com

WORKMAN is a registered trademark of Workman Publishing Co., Inc.

HISTORY and the H logo are registered trademarks of A&E
Television Networks, LLC.

Printed in China
First printing October 2020

10 9 8 7 6 5 4 3 2 1

CONTENTS

INTRODUCTION

· ·

I WAS IN ELEVENTH GRADE WHEN I SAW IT. In Mrs. Sherman's history class. She walked to the front of the room, flicked the switch on the rolling TV, and put on a movie for us.

The movie? The title is long gone from my memory, but the content will never leave: It was a documentary. About the assassination of JFK.

To this day, I can tell you exactly where I sat in Mrs. Sherman's eleventh-grade class. That's how much the film burned its way into my head. I still remember watching it. It wasn't some crazy conspiracy film. It was sensible and logical. It asked reasonable questions and pointed out the holes in the official government story.

I sat there wide-eyed as the black-and-white images flickered on screen. Today, with the Internet, the movement of such information seems far less impressive. But to me . . . in eleventh grade . . . I couldn't believe it. There it was: someone questioning whether our own American government had been *lying to us*. It was like someone kicking at the foundation of my brain.

Still, I can't say I'd never seen anything like it before. One of my father's favorite movies was *All the President's Men*. He wasn't a political guy. I think he just liked Robert Redford and Dustin Hoffman kicking ass and acting tough.

ABOVE

THE KENNEDY ASSASSINATION
For many, Walter Cronkite's announcement of the death of President John F. Kennedy on November 22, 1963, was one of the most unforgettable moments in history.

So when I was thirteen, we used to watch it together—over and over—since back then, having cable TV meant that HBO played the same movie fifteen times a day.

So yes, I'd seen Redford and Hoffman accuse Nixon and his Plumbers of being liars. But to me, JFK was different.

Watergate was a few crooks and a selfish egomaniac of a president. But JFK? It just seemed . . . bigger. To break into an office building required only a few guys. But to kill a president? And then to kill Oswald? And to have Jack Ruby know where to be at the exact right moment? The only way to pull that off was if . . .

My God, how big was this thing? (I was in eleventh grade. Everything back then seemed mind-blowing.)

No question, though, that's the moment that changed my life. Did it make me a conspiracy nut? No. Indeed, to this day, I think if you blame *everything* on the government, you're not just wrong, you're being reckless. It's as silly as blaming everything on the Freemasons, or the Illuminati, or insert-bad-guy-here. But I do believe that someone must ask the hard questions, especially of our elected officials as well as powerful people who become members of so-called secret societies. Remember: Governments don't lie. People lie. And if you want the real story, you need to find out more about those people.

Over the years, I've been contacted by the family of John Wilkes Booth, by former U.S. presidents, and (of course) by the Freemasons. In my thrillers, I've taken readers into the secret labyrinth below the U.S. Capitol (it's real), the hidden tunnel below the White House (also real—it's a bomb shelter),

and even to the secret entrance below the Lincoln Memorial (did you really think when presidents arrive for a visit, they just run up the front steps?).

Those stories are what led to my TV show, *Decoded*. At the time, the HISTORY network told me that if I gave them a list of my favorite historical mysteries, they'd give me a team to help solve them. From there, Buddy Levy, Christine McKinley, Scott Rolle, and our amazing producers and crew have become true family. Together, we've explored some of the greatest conspiracies (and myths) that history has to offer.

To me, history is a giant game of telephone. What's vital is finding the first whisper. Yet of all the questions people ask us about conspiracies, the number one is simply this: Which is your favorite?

And so, this book. Inside, you'll see our favorites, counting down from the mysteries surrounding the Lincoln assassination, to the search for Confederate gold, to the existence of UFOs, to . . . well . . . like I said, you'll see.

As always, our goal is to show you the facts presented by both sides. We'll give you our theories—plus the sensible and logical questions to ask—and then you decide who you believe.

As for those who want the full solutions to every one of these mysteries, let me say it now: Don't write me letters asking for those answers. In some of the chapters, you'll see an answer. In others, you'll get the facts as they exist. Anyone who promises you *all* the answers is forgetting that there's a reason these are the greatest conspiracies and mysteries of all time.

On the very first day we started filming *Decoded*, one of the producers said to me, "On shows like this, the fewer facts you have, the more scary music you play." We decided right there, we didn't want to be one of those shows. And yes, we may have our share of scary music, but when it comes to *The 10 Greatest Conspiracies of All Time*—and the stories in here—we've stuck to one motto: The scariest story of all is always the true story.

Show me your favorite conspiracy and I'll show you who you are. Y'know what that means? It means you're about to find out a great deal about yourself. Just like I did on that day in Mrs. Sherman's history class.

See you in the archives.

—Brad Meltzer

THE
10 GREATEST
CONSPIRACIES
OF ALL TIME

JOHN WILKES BOOTH: WAS LINCOLN'S ASSASSIN APPREHENDED?

WHAT IF I TOLD YOU that after murdering President Abraham Lincoln, the most famous assassin in American history lived for 40 more years?

We all know the story: In 1865, on a Friday night at Ford's Theatre, John Wilkes Booth killed our 16th president with a single bullet to the back of his head. Instantly becoming America's most wanted man, Booth jumped from the presidential balcony and fled on horseback across Maryland and Virginia. But some speculate that the history books—which tell us that Booth was shot 12 days later at Garrett's farm near Port Royal, Virginia—are flat-out *wrong*.

Some believe Booth didn't die that night. They claim he was actually acting on behalf of the Confederate Secret Service, who then aided him in his escape. They argue the man killed at Garrett's barn was

actually a look-alike, a patsy used to throw off Union soldiers. What's even more amazing: This is just one of *three* plausible theories of Booth's escape. If there's even the slightest possibility John Wilkes Booth was able to escape the law and live as a fugitive for another 40 years, I want to know what happened.

It's time to decode John Wilkes Booth.

THE HISTORY

IT WAS GOOD FRIDAY. On April 14, 1865, less than a week after Robert E. Lee surrendered to Ulysses S. Grant at Appomattox, Virginia, President and Mrs. Lincoln made plans to attend the play *Our American Cousin* starring Laura Keene at Ford's Theatre in Washington, DC.

John Wilkes Booth, 26, a handsome, well-known stage actor—think of him as sort of the Brad Pitt of his day—made his own plans for the theater that night. And those plans involved a .44 caliber Derringer. Booth had a dark side: He was an obsessed, fanatical supporter of the Confederate cause (see Exhibit 10A, page 5, a letter Booth left with his brother-in-law). Upon learning that President and Mrs. Lincoln would be attending a performance by renowned actress Laura Keene in the popular comedy *Our American Cousin* at Ford's Theatre in Washington, Booth decided to exact revenge for the Union victory by assassinating Lincoln.

Ford's Theatre was the perfect place for Booth to stage his final performance. As a famous actor, Booth was friends with the owner; he had been in the theater's inaugural play—he even got his mail delivered there. Booth knew the place inside out. This was

home turf. On the night he shot President Lincoln, he didn't even try to conceal his identity. He walked in the front door while the performance was still in progress, said hello to the people who recognized him, and then made his way to the hallway outside the president's private box.

Presidential security back then was nothing like it is today. Lincoln generally traveled with one or two guards, and conveniently, on this night, the man who was supposed to be guarding the door to the box wasn't even there. He left the theater to get a drink with some of his friends. So Booth peered through the peephole in the door (that he's said to have drilled earlier that day) to see inside. There was no guard inside the president's box—just Lincoln, his wife, and another couple. Booth had even memorized the play. He waited until the big laugh line: "Don't know the manners of good society, eh? Well, I guess I know enough to turn you inside out, old gal—you sockdologizing old man-trap."

If Will Ferrell delivered that line today, you would hear crickets. But in 1865, it brought the house down. When the big joke hit and everyone laughed, all Booth had to do was open the unlocked door, walk up behind the president,

and shoot him. His deed done, Booth stabbed a military officer who tried to stop him as he leaped from the box to the stage, 11 feet below.

Landing hard, Booth rose and delivered the last line he would ever speak onstage, the most famous line of his life. *"Sic semper tyrannis!"* he cried, the Latin phrase making clear Booth's sentiments: Thus always to tyrants!

Chaos erupted throughout the theater. Some say Booth broke his leg when he landed. On pure adrenaline, Booth ran out the stage door, mounted his waiting horse, and galloped into the night. History tells us that two weeks later, John Wilkes Booth was surrounded in a Virginia barn and killed by Union troops.

CASE CLOSED?

BUT FOR DECADES Booth's family members have offered a different version of events. Joanne Hulme, a distant relative of John Wilkes Booth, claims when she was a little girl, her mother shared with her the truth about how Booth died: "They're gonna say that he died in a barn. He did not die in a barn. He lived for many, many years."

Booth, along with David Herold, a confidant and fellow Confederate sympathizer, fled on horseback through Maryland into Virginia. They were traveling at high speed, covering 14 miles in a matter of two hours, pausing to collect previously hidden weapons and supplies from the Surratt house, a tavern in Clinton, Maryland. Booth never got off his horse, and probably wasn't there for more than five minutes. But he did have enough time to boast that he had just killed the president of the United States. And why wouldn't he spike that football? Booth thought he was a hero. He believed he had done the Confederacy a favor.

Herold and Booth raced from Surratt's and headed south another 14 miles to Waldorf, Maryland. But this time, it took them four hours instead of two. The pain from his broken leg must have been killing Booth, and they were forced to stop at the home of Dr. Samuel Mudd.

Dr. Mudd set his leg, and it was here that some say Booth took the first steps toward assuming a brand-new identity—shaving his mustache and maybe even coloring his hair. He was officially on the run.

"This country was formed for the white not for the black man. And looking upon African slavery from the same stand-point, as held by those noble framers of our Constitution, I for one, have ever considered it, one of the greatest blessings (both for themselves and us) that God ever bestowed upon a favored nation."

John Wilkes Booth
November, 1864

ABOVE
EXHIBIT 10A
Booth's fanatical letter to his brother-in-law.

Booth and Herold left Dr. Mudd's in the morning. The manhunt for Booth was on. And he already had a $100,000 price on his head. (See Exhibit 10B, page 8. That's a $1.3 million reward, today.) So Booth and Herold spent several days trekking through the forest and swamp, making their way south to friendlier territory. They arrived at Garrett's farm near Port Royal, Virginia, on April 24.

This is the fork in the road.

The belief has always been that Booth was killed in Garrett's barn two nights later by Union soldiers, but there are a lot of people who believe that Booth was never at Garrett's barn and that if he was there, it was only briefly.

So who was in that barn? Lincoln assassination scholar Joan Chaconas believes the play-by-play went something like this:

Twenty-six Union soldiers have Booth and Herold surrounded in the barn. Herold starts freaking out. He wants to surrender. Booth is very comfortable being "onstage" alone. So Booth kicks Herold out of the barn. Herold emerges and is immediately taken into custody.

He will be tried and hanged within ten weeks.

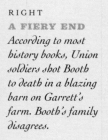

RIGHT

A FIERY END

According to most history books, Union soldiers shot Booth to death in a blazing barn on Garrett's farm. Booth's family disagrees.

Now the soldiers demand Booth surrender. Two words: *No. Way.*

For Booth, this is the performance of a lifetime. He will *not* leave the stage. One of the soldiers sets fire to the back of the barn in an attempt to flush Booth out. Another Union soldier spots Booth inside the barn and fires a shot — hitting him in the back of the neck. Booth is dragged out of the barn. As Booth lies dying, Herold asks a Union army lieutenant, Edward Doherty, "Who was that man that was shot in there? Who was he?"

"Well, you know very well who that was," Doherty says.

"No, I don't know who that was," Herold responds. "He said his name was *Boyd*. He told me his name was *Boyd*. I didn't know it was *Booth*."

Now here's what doesn't make sense. Why would Herold say Booth's name was Boyd? He's been captured. There's nothing to gain. And more important — who is *Boyd*? Is it possible that he's some sort of patsy placed there to take the fall for Booth? There's even speculation the body dragged out of Garrett's barn doesn't even *look* like John Wilkes Booth.

Booth researcher Nathan Orlowek maintains that it's impossible that the

WASHINGTON, DC

FORD'S THEATRE

VIRGINIA

SURRATT HOUSE

HOME OF DR. MUDD

MARYLAND

GARRETT'S FARM

man killed in that barn was John Wilkes Booth: "Three different witnesses said that the man killed in the barn had reddish hair, even though it's a known fact that John Wilkes Booth had jet-black hair, and Dr. May [Booth's doctor] says the body looked much older than the John Wilkes Booth he knew in life and was freckled." Orlowek believes Booth left Garrett's barn two days before the Union army got there. And he thinks it was in everyone's interest for it to be believed that John Wilkes Booth was killed. The reward money offered for Booth's head was over the top. And the political pressure was *huge*. We've got to remember that the country was in complete chaos at this point. The war was over, but the Confederacy was still alive in spirit. The nation was so unstable that all the pressure was on Secretary of War Edwin Stanton to bring Lincoln's assassin to justice.

And y'see that? Now we've got motive.

With the eyes of an entire nation on him, there's just no way to understand the lengths

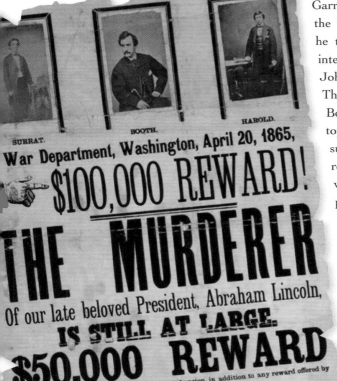

SURRAT.   BOOTH.   HAROLD.

War Department, Washington, April 20, 1865,

$100,000 REWARD!

THE MURDERER

Of our late beloved President, Abraham Lincoln,

IS STILL AT LARGE.

$50,000 REWARD

Will be paid by this Department for his apprehension, in addition to any reward offered by Municipal Authorities or State Executives.

$25,000 REWARD

Will be paid for the apprehension of JOHN H. SURRATT, one of Booth's Accomplices.

$25,000 REWARD

Will be paid for the apprehension of David C. Harold, another of Booth's accomplices.

LIBERAL REWARDS will be paid for any information that shall conduce to the arrest of either of the above-named criminals, or their accomplices.

All persons harboring or secreting the said persons, or either of them, or aiding or assisting their concealment or escape, will be treated as accomplices in the murder of the President and the attempted assassination of the Secretary of State, and shall be subject to trial before a Military Commission and the punishment of DEATH.

that Stanton may have gone to close this case. And knowing that the nation needed Lincoln's killer brought to justice so that it could survive as a united country, here's the key question: Did Stanton place a Booth look-alike at Garrett's farm? Orlowek's most compelling piece of evidence comes from John P. Simonton, who served in the Office of the Judge Advocate General of the War Department for 43 years. In his statement, Simonton claimed, "I studied the evidence in this case and found no definite proof that John Wilkes Booth was ever captured."

ABOVE
A DEAD RINGER
With a change of hair color, James W. Boyd bears a striking resemblance to John Wilkes Booth.

WHO WAS BOYD?

THE NATIONAL ARCHIVES IN WASHINGTON, DC, currently have a service record for Captain James W. Boyd, a Confederate soldier in the Sixth Tennessee Infantry. He was a Union prisoner of war. Back then, Prisoner Boyd was directed by Secretary of War Edwin Stanton to be transferred to Washington, DC. Why would Stanton want James Boyd in DC? It turns out Boyd was actually a spy for the Union. His job was to inform the North about Confederate smuggling operations in Tennessee. And Boyd's paper trail goes cold at a critical time: He disappears from any records after February 15, 1865—two months before Lincoln's assassination. But also within the National Archives resides a photograph of James W. Boyd—and when placed side by side with a photo of Booth, the resemblance is undeniable: Except for hair color, James Boyd is a dead ringer for John Wilkes Booth. Was Boyd summoned to DC by Stanton to be the fall guy? Was he to be inserted into the barn that night

*Edwin Stanton was
under enormous
political, social, and
public pressure to bring
Lincoln's assassin to
justice.*

undercover so he could become Booth? It's a wild theory, but remember: If Stanton's covering this up, it also means Stanton needs a body. And speaking of the body, wait until you read what went down during Booth's autopsy.

According to Jan Herman, a naval historian who has studied the autopsy records of John Wilkes Booth, Booth's body was brought from Garrett's farm to the USS *Montauk*, a monitor-class ironclad ship. There were 13 people present for the autopsy, all connected to the War Department or the Navy Department—including a photographer. Herman claims only one photograph of Booth's body was taken, and that negative was handed over to a detective who turned it in to Secretary of War Stanton as soon as it was snapped. Herman believes the negative has been lost over the decades—perhaps intentionally. Even more intriguing: Booth's family was not even allowed to see the body. And even more intriguing than that: There were other apprehended Lincoln assassin conspirators being held prisoner aboard the USS *Montauk*—but none of them was brought up on deck to identify Booth. Prominent District of Columbia surgeon Dr. John Frederick May, who was summoned to identify the body, and who actually operated on Booth years before, told the assembled witnesses, "This body doesn't look anything like Booth. I don't recall Booth being freckled. I don't recall him being as old as this gentleman."

But according to Herman, Dr. May felt pressured to go along with the idea that it was Booth's body. She suggests Dr. May went along with the investigation because he didn't want to risk being implicated in any part of the assassination. So under immense pressure, Dr. May signed off that the body was, in fact, Booth. Herman believes these details reveal a very sloppy identification of Booth—one that might not hold up to scrutiny. But she also believes there are three little letters that could potentially blow this investigation wide open: DNA.

During Booth's autopsy, the cervical vertebrae and a small section of his spinal cord were removed. Those pieces of Booth's body are still hanging around. They currently reside at the National Museum of Health and Medicine in Maryland. Herman believes that if you extract a DNA sample of the Booth tissue from the vertebrae and spinal cord . . . and then you compare those samples with DNA taken from a partial exhumation of Edwin Booth—John's brother— that would provide indisputable evidence as to whether it was actually John Wilkes Booth who was shot and killed at Garrett's barn on April 26, 1865.

Nothing would be stronger than an actual DNA comparison, and now that's possible. All that would be necessary is to get permission to test the piece of bone in Maryland and compare it to the sample of Booth's brother Edwin's body in Massachusetts. In recent years, Booth descendants have taken steps to do just that. But until the courts allow that to happen, the question remains unanswered. Still, we have to ask: Why would they possibly deny what would give them the truth?

BELOW
SHIPBOARD
AUTOPSY
Booth's body was brought from Garrett's farm to the USS Montauk, *a monitor-class ironclad ship, where 13 people were present for the autopsy.*

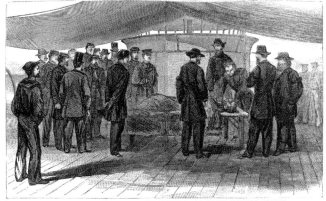

POST-MORTEM EXAMINATION OF BOOTH'S BODY ON BOARD THE MONITOR *MONTAUK*.

WHERE DID HE GO?

IF JOHN WILKES BOOTH CONTINUED TO LIVE, there should be evidence of that. But where did he go? One theory is that when Booth realized Jefferson Davis wasn't going to throw a parade for him and that he was basically screwed forever, he adopted an alias. Interviewing historians about various theories, we found two different aliases that have enough credible evidence surrounding them to investigate: John St. Helen and John B. Wilkes. That gives us three possibilities: One is that Booth assumed Boyd's identity (though there are no records of Boyd after Lincoln's assassination). Another is Booth assumed the alias of John B. Wilkes and fled the country. And the final is that, as a patriot who was willing to kill for his country, Booth possibly stayed in the United States and lived out his days in West Texas under the alias John St. Helen.

Chuck Huppert, a John Wilkes Booth researcher who believes Booth pulled off a 19th-century version of identity theft, says Booth was introduced to an Englishman in Indiana named John B. Wilkes who was born in Sheffield, England, in 1822. Huppert claims Booth stole Wilkes's identity and traveled to India posing as the Englishman, where he remained until his death in 1883. Huppert believes John B. Wilkes actually returned to the United States in 1873, and has a photograph of Wilkes he says was taken during that visit. The man in the photograph looks *identical* to John Wilkes Booth. Huppert doubles down on his theory with a will that he says John B. Wilkes wrote in India in 1883 — *18 years* after Booth's alleged death. The will contains special bequests to people who were friends and family of John Wilkes Booth:

- $25,000 to Ogarita Rosalie Wilkes, "natural heir of my body." Ogarita Rosalie Wilkes is Booth's daughter by his wife, Izola Mills Darcy Booth, who is said to have married John Wilkes Booth in 1859.

- $25,000 to Mary Louise Turner, "natural heir of my body." Turner is another daughter of Booth, this time by Ella Turner, who was at the time of the assassination John Wilkes Booth's mistress.

There's also a bequest to Henry Johnson:

- $1,000 a year to Henry Johnson, "a free Negro . . . to whom I owe my very life." Johnson was Booth's personal valet, who later escaped to Harpers Ferry, West Virginia.

One cannot help but ask: "Why in the world would John Byron Wilkes be giving money to John Wilkes Booth's wife?"

NOW BE IT KNOWN TO ALL WHO COME INTO THESE PRESENCE, THAT I,

JOHN BYRON WILKES

BEING OF SOUND MIND, IN GOOD SPIRITS, AND IN GRACE WITH GOD, BELIEVING

DEATH TO BE IMMINENT, IN THE PRESENCE OF GOD AND THESE WITNESSES, DO

HEREWITH DESIGN, RECORD, AND PUBLISH THIS, MY LAST WILL AND TESTIMENT,

TO WIT :

FIRSTLY, TO OGARITA ROSALIE WILKES, ____ HEIR OF MY BODY, I BEQUEATH

THE SUM OF TWENTY FIVE THOUS___ _____ UNITED STATES CURRENCY.

SECONDLY, TO HARRY JEROME STEVENSON   BEQUESTH THE SUM OF TWENTY FIVE

THOUSAND DOLLARS IN UNITED STATES CURRENCY.

THIRDLY, TO MARY LOUISE TURNER, NATURAL HEIR OF MY BODY, I BEQUESTH

THE SUM OF TWENTY FIVE THOUSAND DOLLARS IN UNITED STATES CURRENCY, AND

APPOINT JOHN HARDMAN AS HER TRUSTEE UNTIL SHE SHALL HAVE REACHED THE

AGE OF THIRTY YEARS OR SHALL HAVE MARRIED, WHICHEVER SHALL HAVE OCCURRED

FIRST.

FOURTHLY, TO SARAH KATHERINE SCOTT, NATURAL HEIR OF MY BODY, I BEQUESTH

THE SUM OF TWENTY FIVE THOUSAND DOLLARS IN UNITED STATES CURRENCY AND

APPOINT ANDREW POTTER AS HER TRUSTEE UNTIL SHE SHALL HAVE REACHED THE

AGE OF THIRTY YEARS OR SHALL HAVE MARRIED, WHICHEVER SHALL HAVE OCCURRED

FIRST.

FIFTHLY, TO IZOLA MARTHA STEVENSON I BEQUESTH THE SUM OF FIFTEEN THOUSAND

DOLLARS IN UNITED STATES CURRENCY.

SIXTHLY, TO ELLA TURNER I BEQUESTH THE SUM OF FIFTEEN THOUSAND DOLLARS IN

UNITED STATES CURRENCY.

SEVENTHLY, TO KATE M. SCOTT I BEQUEATH THE SUM OF FIFTEEN THOUSAND DOLLARS

IN UNITED STATES CURRENCY.

EIGHTLY, TO HENRY JOHNSON, A FREE NEGRO RESIDING IN THE CITY OF NEW YORK, IN GRATEFUL APPRECIATION FOR GREAT AND FAITHFUL SERVICE AND TO WHOM I OWE MY VERY LIFE, I BEQUESTH THE SUM OF ONE THOUSAND DOLLARS IN UNITED STATES CURRENCY EACH YEAR THAT HE SHALL HEREAFTER LIVE TO BE PAID EACH YEAR ON THE ANNIVERSARY OF HIS BIRTH AS HE SHALL STATE IT.

NINETHLY, TO SARAH JOHNSON, A FREE NEGRO WOMAN RESIDING IN BOSTON, I BEQUEATH THE SUM OF FIVE HUNDRED DO̶̶̶̶̶ ̶̶̶̶̶ IN UNITED STATES CURRENCY EACH YEAR FOR THE REMAINDER OF ̶̶̶̶̶̶̶̶̶̶

TENTHLY, TO MY BELOVED WIFE AND ̶̶̶̶̶̶̶̶̶ ELIZABETH MARSHALL WILKES, I BEQUEATH THE REMAINDER OF MY BELONGINGS, REAL AND PERSONAL, WITH THE STIPULATION THAT ALL MY DEBTS BE FIRST PAID FROM MY ESTATE, AND FURTHER, THAT TWO THOUSAND POUNDS STERLING BE PAID TO EACH OF ELIZABETH MARSHALL WILKES DAUGHTERS.

ELEVENTHLY, I APPOINT ROGER MCCRACKEN AS MY EXECUTOR AND TRUSTEE AND DIRECT THAT IMMEDIATELY AFTER MY DEMISE, HE SHALL PAY ALL LEGITIMATE INDEBTEDNESS AGAINST ME AND MY ESTATE AND SHALL THEN AS CONSISTANT WITH GOOD PRACTICE AND CROWN LAW, DISTRIBUTE THE RESIDUE WITH ALL DUE DISPATCH AND MAY GOD BLESS HIM.

TWELFTHLY, ROGER MCCRACKEN SHALL BE PAID THE SUM OF TWO THOUSAND POUNDS STERLING FOR HIS EFFORTS IN MY BEHALF AND SHALL HAVE FULL AUTHORITY TO RETAIN, HIRE, AND DIRECT ALL THOSE PERSONS AND PARTIES THAT HE SHALL FIND NECESSARY AND DESIRABLE TO AID HIM IN THE PERFORMANCE OF HIS ASSIGNED TASK. EXECUTED AND WITNESSED THIS TWELFTH DAY OF SEPTEMBER THIS YEAR OF OUR LORD, EIGHTEEN HUNDRED AND EIGHTY THREE, AT BOMBAY, INDIA.

S/ JOHN BYRON WILKES (SEAL)

WITNESS :

S/ GEORGE FORRESTER   (SEAL)

S/ EDWIN HENSON   (SEAL)

PREVIOUS PAGE
EXHIBIT 10C
*The unsigned will of
John Byron Wilkes*

Huppert offers a simple explanation, "It wasn't John B. Wilkes that was really writing this will."

I'll admit this is compelling evidence that it was actually John Wilkes Booth writing his will as John B. Wilkes. But here's where it all falls apart: Look at Exhibit 10C (pages 14 and 15). The will *isn't* signed. If it was, anyone would be able to analyze the handwriting and compare it against other known Booth signatures. But without a signature, or any other way to authenticate the will, and no way to authenticate the photograph of Wilkes, this theory that John Wilkes Booth lived out his years as Englishman John B. Wilkes remains just that: a theory.

That leaves John St. Helen.

Em Turner Chitty is the daughter of the late Dr. Arthur Ben Chitty. Arthur was a historiographer at the University

of the South and one of the main proponents of the theory that John Wilkes Booth used John St. Helen as an alias. Dr. Chitty passed away in 2002, and his daughter has now become the family Booth expert. Chitty contends Booth actually arrived in Franklin County, Tennessee, in 1872. There he fell in love with and married a local girl named Louisa Payne. According to Chitty, when Booth confessed to Louisa that he would love her forever—and, oh yeah, that he also assassinated the 16th president of the United States—Louisa was unfazed. Fazed she became, however, when Louisa found out she had married a man under the wrong name. Louisa freaked out so much, she demanded that they go back to the courthouse and get remarried using Booth's real name. And according to Chitty, the Franklin County Courthouse marriage register clearly shows John W. Booth's signature, on February 24, 1872—*seven years* after the assassination.

But what raises my eyebrow most is when 90-year-old Juanita Keele, a living relative of Louisa Payne, decided it was time to talk: "My grandmother's sister married John Wilkes Booth. . . . They were married before he told her."

Keele went on to say that Booth went by the name John St. Helen until he came clean to Louisa. As newly-weds, Booth and Louisa moved to Memphis, where she grew homesick. Louisa returned home to her family. Booth told her he would come back, but he never did. The identity of Louisa Payne's husband remained a closely held family secret before Keele decided to come forward. When asked how her family felt being "married to the Mob," Juanita said, "It was not to be talked about outside the family."

So why was she willing to talk about it now?

FACING PAGE
REMARRIED AS BOOTH
Marriage certificate from the second ceremony that Louisa Payne insisted upon after she learned that her husband, John St. Helen, was really John Wilkes Booth.

"Well, at my age, I've decided everybody's dead that mattered, you know, that would have been hurt by it, so I'll tell it."

So where did John St. Helen go from Memphis? Mary Bates Wehbi, granddaughter of lawyer Finis L. Bates, believes her grandfather was a confidant of John Wilkes Booth in Granbury, Texas—but he was calling himself John St. Helen at the time. According to Wehbi, Bates received news that St. Helen was dying and sent for him. He needed to make a deathbed confession. He told Bates how he had escaped. Wehbi retells the story: "As he made the confession, my grandfather began to think that no man would make a deathbed confession this serious if he were not the real person."

According to Bates, John St. Helen did not die that day. He actually recovered, left Texas, and settled in Enid, Oklahoma, assuming a new alias: David E. George. And here's the crazy part: The name appears to be code. Two of Booth's coconspirators were *David* Herold and *George E.* Atzerodt: David E. George. It's either a sly reference to Booth's true identity—or just a guy with two first names.

In 1903, Bates saw an obituary indicating that a man from Enid, Oklahoma, had confessed to being John

Can it be proven beyond a shadow of a doubt that Booth was neither John St. Helen nor John B. Wilkes? The only way to know for sure is to exhume Edwin Booth's body and do the DNA testing.

Wilkes Booth. The body was in the mortuary waiting to be claimed. So what did Bates do? He makes the trip to Enid to identify the body, and sure enough, it was his friend John St. Helen—or John Wilkes Booth.

MUMMIES

THE DAVID E. GEORGE PART is one of the wildest parts of the story. The man committed suicide by drinking arsenic. The arsenic, combined with his embalming fluids, mummified his body. So when Finis Bates arrived to identify the body, they gave him the mummy because no one else claimed it.

Can we just stop here? One: We have a mummified body that people think is John Wilkes Booth. Two: People are giving away mummies!

Over the years, Bates even tried to sell it a few times. He actually offered it to Henry Ford for $1,000, but ultimately, it ended up (like so many mummies) in his garage. When Bates died in 1923, his wife sold it to a traveling circus. The mummy toured the United States for almost 50 years before vanishing in the early 1970s.

Are you paying attention to this? We've got people paying to see a mummified body that they think is John Wilkes Booth? *This is officially the greatest Abraham Lincoln story of all time.*

Here's what we know: There is evidence that John Wilkes Booth may have not been killed at Garrett's barn, but is that evidence airtight? Can it be proven beyond a shadow of a doubt that Booth

BELOW
MUMMIFIED
ASSASSIN
Embalming fluids, combined with the arsenic he drank to end his life, mummified the body of John St. Helen aka John Wilkes Booth.

was neither John St. Helen nor John B. Wilkes? The only way to really know for sure is to exhume Edwin Booth's body and do the DNA testing.

The problem is, exhuming a dead body isn't as easy as it used to be.

When the Booth family petitioned in 1994 to have Booth's body exhumed and its DNA tested against his brother Edwin's, the state's attorney in Baltimore originally said it was OK to exhume John Wilkes Booth's remains. But then somebody appealed that decision to the courts and it went to a judge for a decision. The judge wrote that "the alleged remains of John Wilkes Booth were buried in an unknown location some 126 years ago, and there is evidence that three infant siblings are buried on top of John Wilkes Booth's remains. There may be severe water damage to the Booth burial plot, and there are no dental records available for comparison. Thus, an identification may be inconclusive. So the above reasons, coupled with the unreliability of the petitioner's less than convincing escape/cover-up theory gives rise to the conclusion that there is no compelling reason for exhumation."

ADDITIONALLY, one of the objections to examining John Wilkes Booth's body was that it would have been out of the ground for as long as six weeks

after exhumation. That was more than 15 years ago. Given today's technology, there's a far easier workaround. All we need is a sample from Booth's brother, Edwin, and access to that bone in the museum in Maryland. A DNA test is our best shot at solving the John Wilkes Booth case once and for all. If we want to close this chapter in our history, we'll need to compare the samples that we know exist with a DNA sample from Booth's brother, Edwin.

This test is either going to show that they're *brothers*. Or that they're *strangers*.

But without that, all we have is a great story of a famous actor who leaped from the stage to legend by pulling off the role of his life—hiding his own identity and hiding from history. So until we force the hands of the powers that be and test that DNA, we'll never know for sure whether John Wilkes Booth died in 1865 or not.

CONFEDERATE GOLD: STOLEN TREASURE OR HIDDEN WEALTH OF A NEW CONFEDERACY?

WHAT IF I TOLD YOU that almost $20 million in gold and silver simply disappeared at the end of the Civil War?

It was early April 1865. Confederate President Jefferson Davis decided to gather the riches of his government and flee to the Deep South, where he hoped it would be safe.

Over the next two months, the rebel gold traveled by train and wagon across Dixie. Along the way, Davis hid massive caches of gold and silver in the hopes that the Confederacy would one day rise again. Some say the group that he charged with stashing the rebel gold was the Knights of the Golden Circle—the KGC—a secret society founded in the 1850s to promote the interests of the South. The KGC used a code made up of an elaborate system of signs and symbols to mark the hiding spots.

To this day, most of the money is still missing. Indeed, 150 years ago, it was hidden *so well* that modern technology *still* can't find it.

Could mysterious carvings and symbols throughout the South be clues to the location of the vanished treasure?

Most important: Who took the Confederate gold? Was it stolen—or was it *hidden*? And where is it now?

When it comes to the most tragic period in our nation's history, *this* is its greatest mystery.

EARLY APRIL 1865

THE AMERICAN CIVIL WAR was drawing to its close. After four terrible, bloody, devastating years, the Confederacy was defeated but had not yet surrendered. Battles still raged, although Union forces were poised to overrun Richmond, the Confederate capital and the home to the executive mansion, which served as a Confederate White House.

The remnants of Robert E. Lee's once powerful army, barely two dozen miles away at Petersburg, could not hold back the Northern forces for long.

In church on Sunday morning, April 2, Jefferson Davis, president of the Confederate States of America, was no doubt praying for some sort of military miracle. It was not to be. Even before the Sunday services were concluded, Davis was informed that Lee's defensive line at Petersburg had failed. The Yankees were within 24 miles of the Confederate capital. Federal troops would be inside the city limits of Richmond at any time. The city had to be evacuated.

FACING PAGE TOP
CONFEDERATE FLIGHT
With the Yankees at the gates of Richmond in April 1865, Jefferson Davis boarded a train whose locomotive pulled Confederate treasure as well as Confederate leaders.

FACING PAGE BOTTOM
DESTINATION DANVILLE
After a harrowing delay, Davis's train sped out of Richmond just before midnight, bound for Danville, Virginia.

Desperately clinging to hope, Davis prevailed upon Lee to rally his troops for one more heroic stand. He needed enough time for the Confederacy's government and, crucially, the remains of its treasury, to escape the oncoming Federal troops. If the treasury could be preserved, maybe the Confederacy wouldn't be dead.

The Confederate treasury amounted to about $10 million today. The Virginia bank assets worked out to around $9 million today. That meant Davis had approximately $19 million. He knew it. Between the gold and silver coins, some gold bullion, and a fair amount of jewelry and precious stones, he had more than enough to finance a new army. That was his hope.

Still, Davis needed time to turn his hope into a plan. He needed that day he asked Lee to give him.

But Lee couldn't make such a promise. The only thing he could guarantee to Davis was the rest of Sunday to make his escape. By eight o'clock that evening, Lee and what remained of his army would themselves be falling back. Richmond was lost.

With the final few hours Davis had left, he arranged for at least two—and possibly as many as nine—trains to steam south

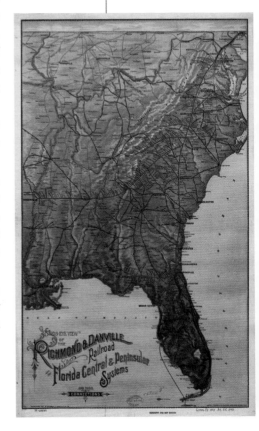

CHECK YOUR BALANCE

So how much money are we talking about? What was the real value of the Confederate treasure?

Reports vary, with a few claiming that there never was any treasure. But according to most sources, the amounts removed from Richmond were substantial, including:

- U.S. silver coins

- U.S. gold coins

- $200,000 in Mexican silver coins packed into 39 kegs

- Gold bullion

- Jewelry and precious stones

The U.S. coins consisted of $327,000 in specie. Because the coins were U.S. currency (the Confederacy did not mint its own coins), the money retained its value, unlike Confederate paper money, which was already nearly worthless.

So how much was it all worth?

Best estimates put it at more than $19 million in today's currency. More than enough to pick a few fights — and potentially start another war.

from the capital. One would bear the president, his cabinet, and other officials. Another would carry the treasury of the Confederacy, as well as the assets of six Richmond banks. With an eye focused on both history and the future, the archives and papers related to the government would be evacuated as well.

That night, they missed the eight o'clock deadline, but by midnight, the trains had left the falling capital, making the best speed possible on the last of the Confederacy's southbound rail lines. Their destination? Danville, Virginia — just above the North Carolina border.

Outside Danville, one of the trains met with disaster as a boxcar collapsed, causing the engine to derail. Five soldiers were said to have died in the crash, although only two of the bodies were identified. As rescuers sought to salvage whatever could be removed from the wreckage — and transport it by wagon train we find the beginnings of the legend of Confederate gold buried in or near Danville.

After a formal meeting of the Confederate cabinet — which to many people makes Danville the last capital of the Confederacy — the president and other officials set out for the deeper south, where they'd attempt to hold the government together. Some say that Davis was already looking westward for a new base of power and resurgence.

THE SURRENDER OF GENERAL LEE

He wouldn't find it. Jefferson Davis was captured by Union cavalry in Irwinville, Georgia, on May 10.

But on April 6, the treasure— made up of coins, bullion, jewelry, and precious stones—was all set to be moved. The Confederacy had three days left to live.

The dual journeys south took weeks, during which the fate of the Confederacy was sealed. Lee's battered army finally came to rest in Appomattox, Virginia, northeast of Danville. On April 9, in a comfortable parlor, Ulysses S. Grant and Robert E. Lee signed papers that would bring an end to the Confederacy's most important military force. The opposing generals' signatures effectively ended hostilities between North and South.

The war was over at last; the reunited nation was weary of battles and bloodshed.

But even as the signing took place, the wealth of the Confederate treasury and the assets of the Richmond banks continued to move deeper south, where plans were made to put it in hiding. Soon, the time would be ripe. With the hidden funds, a new war could be fought. The South could rise again.

As for an exact dollar amount, we'll never really know for sure because on April 2, at the same time the treasure was being snuck out of Richmond, portions of it began to disappear almost immediately.

The first losses took place in Danville—some say during the aftermath of the train wreck . . . others say during the time that the treasure train awaited instructions to

ABOVE
WAGON TRAIN
When rail transport failed, the treasure was transferred to wagons.

FACING PAGE
CONFEDERATE SURRENDER
Even as Robert E. Lee surrendered to Ulysses S. Grant at Appomattox, Virginia, on April 9, 1865, some Confederates clung to the hope that the South would rise again.

move farther south. But Danville was far from the last location where the treasure dwindled. In fact, many believe that the disappearances were part of a larger, deliberate plan—a plan that some say involved burying many separate caches of coins and jewelry throughout the South, along the route taken between Danville and the wagon train's ultimate destination: Washington, Georgia, where Jefferson Davis was waiting.

So on April 6, just three days before the surrender at Appomattox, the treasure began to move south once more. And in the course of heading south, the first real accounting of the treasure began.

That accounting revealed that $200,000 had already gone missing. Civil War historian Mark Waters believes that the Mexican silver dollars were removed from the caravan in Danville, though no one knows whether it was stolen or purposely hidden as part of a larger overall plan.

"What they did with it and where it went, no one has been able to decode, if you will," Waters said.

But when it comes to what happened, here's one argument in favor of the gold being *hidden* rather than *stolen:* That many Mexican silver dollars could have weighed as much as five *tons.* That much weight would've required thieves to be as well equipped with wagons and horses as the Confederates themselves. And the Confederates would have known that the weight of Mexican silver dollars would slow them down as well. So it'd make sense to separate the Mexican silver dollars from the rest of the treasury, perhaps burying it in Danville for later recovery.

"In fact, that's one of the legends of Danville," Waters agreed, "that maybe this has been buried in a cemetery."

THE TREASURE DISAPPEARS

WHEREVER IT IS, STOLEN OR HIDDEN, as the Confederacy was collapsing, all that mattered was keeping the treasury out of Union hands.

The initial plan was to transfer the treasure to Charlotte, North Carolina, where a former U.S. Mint had been commandeered by the Confederacy. But as the wagon train approached Charlotte, it became clear that Union forces were already strong in the region.

At that moment, the Confederate naval officers and midshipmen in charge of transporting the treasure changed their plans, hiding the coins and valuables in casks, barrels, empty ammunition boxes, even flour and sugar bags, then drove southward, hoping to reach Georgia.

Stop by stop, the treasure dwindled. "Rebel gold vanished all across the South," Waters explained. But once again, no one knows the hows or whys. Was the money being stolen—or siphoned off and distributed as part of a larger plan?

Finally, in Washington, Georgia—more than six weeks after fleeing Richmond, and two weeks after Jefferson Davis himself had been captured—the Confederate treasury and other valuables eventually came to rest in a local bank. It wasn't there long. Union forces seized it all.

But here's where the story gets even better: The commander of the Union forces gave the order to move the fortune to the railhead at Abbeville. But despite the forces at his disposal, the commander assigned only five privates and two sergeants to guard the five-wagon caravan.

Guess what happens next?

That's right. On May 24, at the stroke of midnight (when else?), a group of 20 riders reportedly approached the farm near Chennault Plantation, which was where the treasure wagons and their small force of guards had paused for the night.

The robbers were scruffily dressed, making it unclear which side they were on. Some say they were former Confederate soldiers . . . others that they were Union deserters.

Whatever their allegiance, the 20 of them quickly overpowered the paltry guard force. They were so silent, the residents of the nearby farmhouse heard nothing.

But if the robbery was well planned, the raiders forgot one thing: how to escape when you're carrying so many heavy coins. Scrambling, they loaded gold coins into their pockets, saddlebags, and haversacks.

According to historian William C. Davis, some of the robbers even removed their pants, knotted the cuffs, and filled the garments until they could virtually stand upright.

During the robbery, tens of thousands of dollars of gold fell to the ground. After placing the cash-filled pants over the backs of their horses, the robbers made off as quickly and silently as they'd arrived. Their haul? As much as $250,000.

In the hours that followed, the trail was followed by soldiers and local authorities, but according to some residents of Washington, the pursuit was halfhearted at best. While as much as $80,000 of the stolen money was eventually recovered, the majority was never found—and has never been found to this day.

In fact, rumors quickly circulated that some of the so-called pursuers were actually in league with

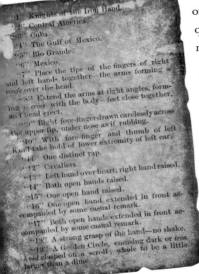

the robbers. It makes sense, especially when you see that the Union commander had such a small group of guards looking out for the treasure . . . and on top of that, that everyone in the region knew that the Confederate treasure was there.

So let's ask the question: Was the poorly guarded treasure train a complete setup—deliberately vulnerable in order to make it easier to rob? And was the robbery itself part of a much larger, carefully orchestrated plan?

To pull off such a plan, you'd need some pretty high-level planners . . . plus people who could keep a secret . . . and most of all, you'd need some amazing hiding places to stash the treasure away.

Indeed, the complexity of the undertaking has led many to speculate that the job was given to an organization whose specialty was secret-keeping . . . and whose commitment to the Southern cause was unquestioned: the secret society known as the Knights of the Golden Circle, or KGC.

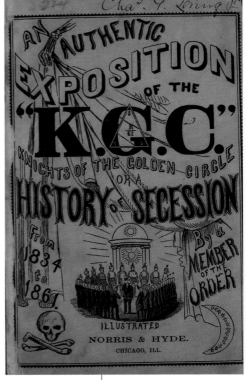

THE KNIGHTS OF THE GOLDEN CIRCLE

THE SECRETIVE KNIGHTS of the Golden Circle were controversial from the start. Supposedly founded on the Fourth of July in Lexington, Kentucky, by Virginia-born

SECRETS OF THE KGC

Once admitted to the Knights of the Golden Circle, members had to swear they would bar anyone who wasn't a moral and upstanding white male (hence, people still call them the precursors to the KKK. Some even say the KGC became the KKK). But the group's real power was hard to gauge because it existed in the shadows. Still, the National Archives has collected some of their secrets.

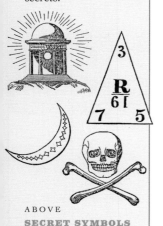

ABOVE

SECRET SYMBOLS
The sentinels of the KGC had their own private language: a combination of letters, symbols, and numerals that, when arranged in certain ways, enabled clandestine communications and also pointed the way to the location of hidden materials. See Exhibit 9A (page 30) for a member identification guide.

physician George W. L. Bickley, the knights were one of the many groups that, during the Civil War, provided an outlet for the anger that was running rampant in the country.

But unlike the Freemasons or other secret societies, who were focused on longtime traditions, the KGC wanted something far more hateful: for the Union to end so they could run their own slave-based society. Their goal was to create a true, physical "golden circle"—with Mexico and the Caribbean—to build a private part of the country where slavery would continue. If that led to breaking up the Union, the KGC was all for it.

Over time, the KGC claimed to have many members in Northern states, as well as throughout the South. But since records and documentation detailing the group's professed purposes were scarce to nonexistent, historians still debate whether they truly had any power. Regardless, at the height of the war, rumors spread that the KGC had penetrated the entire Union. Pennsylvania was said to be overrun with KGC members who were plotting to overthrow the government, capture Washington, DC, and even to kidnap President Abraham Lincoln and cut off his head (depending on who you ask, both John Wilkes Booth and Jesse James were rumored to be KGC members—though good luck on finding the proof).

In the end, regardless of the scope of their power, the KGC had one thing they were incredibly good at: *keeping secrets.*

From its very structure, the KGC was designed to maximize secrecy. Organized into groups called *castles*, these castles were guarded by specially designated *sentinels*—individuals entrusted with the organization's greatest secret:

CRACKING THE KGC CODE

A LITTLE WARNING HERE. Treasure hunter Bob Brewer's system for interpreting hidden KGC signs is a bit complicated. And by complicated, I mean sometimes it can even look a bit crazy. But the bare bones of the system is this: Each sign suggests a distance or a heading that leads to the next sign.

So Brewer draws a line from sign to sign on a topographical map of the area, and where the lines intersect, he'll either find treasure or he'll find another sign that will lead him to the next clue. One of the first codes he cracked was on a Bible Tree.

The trunk of Bob's tree is covered with carvings he spent a lifetime trying to decode. One of them refers to a specific Bible passage—1 Thessalonians 2:3.

Other carvings seem purely symbolic: a cross, a bell, a horse, a bird, and what looks like random numbers and letters. See Exhibit 9B (pages 34 and 35) for the KGC's secret alphabet.

Brewer suspected that each of the 60 carvings was part of a code for something else. The only way to find out was through trial and error. He spent years analyzing the symbols, measuring distances, looking for other nearby signs. But nothing on these trees is what it seems.

According to Brewer, the KGC were masters of misdirection who intentionally loaded their carvings with false leads. They were betting that most treasure hunters would get so frustrated after chasing these bogus clues, they'd give up before they ever found anything. But Bob kept trying. Before long, he had a map full of coordinates that would ultimately lead him to the rebel gold.

Some other typical symbols and treasure marks include:

- Animal: a travel symbol, which—when combined with a directional clue—tells where you should be headed

- Picture of a ghost (bottom left): This means you're looking for a grave.

- A heart or the letter *H* (which stands for heart)

- Numeral: a distance measure telling you how far you need to go or a reference to something you're looking for. (The number *8* might send you to a nearby gazebo. Why that gazebo? It has eight sides, naturally. Top right.)

Again, as you can tell, this isn't a simple process. There are *hundreds* of such symbols, which can produce a near-infinite number of combinations—and a near-infinite number of interpretations.

It calls for a special kind of mind: analytical, experienced, and, some would say, somewhat eccentric (which is a nice way to say *somewhat crazy*).

But in the end, this is a long way from the X MARKS THE SPOT treasure maps of our childhoods.

THE GRAVE

As we followed Bob Brewer on his treasure hunt for Confederate gold, it wasn't the grave itself that caught his interest. It was the misspelling on the tombstone's inscription. Instead of SAYLER'S CREEK, the inscription read SAILOR'S CREEK.

Mistake by the stone carver, right? Not to Brewer. In his eyes, the misspelling was a clue. A clue that formed an anagram: SAILORS.

To Brewer, those letters can be rearranged to spell: RAILS SO.

What's RAILS SO? The letters *so* mean "south." As in, railroad south. Rails to the south.

And what was right nearby that grave? You guessed it. The original tracks and railbed that was used back then. Railroads that were once real helpful in moving the Confederate treasure.

guarding the Confederacy's hidden treasure, generation to generation, over the course of a century.

To understand these sentinels, we spoke to treasure hunter Bob Brewer, coauthor of *Rebel Gold*. Brewer was fortunate in that both his grandfather and uncle were skilled in spotting and interpreting KGC signs, and he learned by carefully watching them when he was young. Brewer said that these sentinels had their own private language: a combination of letters, symbols, and numerals that, when arranged in certain ways, can provide clandestine communications and point the way to the location of hidden materials.

In other words, the KGC had its very own language and system for providing what are essentially map coordinates—and they did it in a way that avoids a customary map.

Why? To protect the treasure, of course. If the details were written on a map, and the map got stolen, so too would the treasure. But with a KGC sentinel, the sentinel stands guard, and the secret stays safe.

The result is that only these so-called sentinels can decode the hidden symbols and "read" the messages the KGC left behind. More than that, though, only sentinels,

or those trained by them, know how to *find* the symbols and their messages.

Why's that? Because the symbols and messages of the KGC aren't just sitting there, printed on a map.

In fact, they're not *printed* at all.

According to Brewer, to make sure these messages would be around for centuries, they're carved into tree trunks, etched into rocks, and even put into deliberate misspellings on certain tombstones.

That's right. When it came to hiding the Confederate treasure, the KGC supposedly used the best hiding spot of all: right in plain sight.

ABOVE ALL, THE SUPPOSED KGC code relies heavily upon biblical chapter and verse, which was chosen because all of its members would've known it well. A cryptic carving might direct the sentinel to a verse in the Bible, and then the interpretation of that would further guide the sentinel—or a knowledgeable treasure hunter—to another symbol, another coordinate, another step on the path to the hidden wealth.

Of course, the very complexity of the system is also one of its greatest flaws. Sentinels, like everyone else, grow old and eventually die. If they die without passing on their special knowledge, the knowledge goes to the grave with them. (Another flaw in the system is that trees age, too: The carving that was at eye level in 1865 could be dozens or more feet higher a few years later. Trees die and are cut down, too, which is why the KGC symbol-carvers often chose sturdy, long-lived, smooth-barked trees, such as holly, for their messages.)

Yet there is something undeniably compelling about watching a treasure hunter and KGC expert like Bob Brewer go about his work, studying a mark on a tree that most of us would overlook and deciding—or divining— that once we're at that eight-sided gazebo, the symbol of a ghost means that we're now looking for a specific grave.

Confused yet? Yeah, so were we. But this cryptic game of hide-and-seek is what makes it one of the greatest historical mysteries. So many of the symbols can be interpreted in so many different ways, there's always the possibility that all

The above is a true coppy of the K.G.C. alpha- bet given me by George Washington Lamb Bickley.

A. A. Urban

we're really looking at is a blank slate onto which *anything* can be read.

But.

Using his ability to interpret KGC symbols—along with a mysterious map-coordinate template that was once owned by a Confederate soldier (and which he overlays onto old maps), Brewer *has found treasure.* As much as $200,000 worth over the past few decades. And he's convinced he'll be able to find more.

Along the way, he's also found more about the role the KGC may have played in the lives of his grandfather and uncle, who showed him his first "treasure tree" when he was a boy.

But when it comes to the actual treasure, what further complicates matters is the possibility that this gold is buried in public cemeteries, such as the Green Hill Cemetery in Danville. The object of intense scrutiny by seekers of Confederate gold, Green Hill Cemetery could well be a prime hiding place for the $200,000 that disappeared a century ago.

In fact, on our outing, Brewer followed a trail of KGC codes and symbols, noting the letter *H* carved into a few places. He insisted we were looking for a "heart"—that the *H* stood for "heart." We kept looking around. There were no hearts. Brewer was still insistent. *Look for the heart!* By then, most of us thought he might be crazy. Until we pulled an old map of the cemetery and—using Brewer's template—saw a heart shape in the cemetery's roads.

From there, Brewer led us to a specific grave, which we then scanned with ground penetrating radar (GPR). A GPR unit does exactly what its name says—scans the territory beneath the surface of the earth and records the bouncebacks of its signals, searching for anomalies.

Sure enough, at the grave in Green Hill Cemetery, there was an anomaly: a mass in the grave that didn't conform to expectations.

What was inside? Was it a hidden cache of gold? Jefferson Davis's frozen head?

Without exhuming the grave, there was just no way to find out. And because Green Hill is a public cemetery, digging it up wasn't going to happen.

Is it any wonder that Brewer was a consultant on the movie *National Treasure*?

OBVIOUSLY, MOST OF US didn't think we'd be finding the lost Confederate gold on our first time out. But it did raise the question: Was the Confederate treasure simply stolen . . . or was it hidden by the KGC as part of a large and complex plan for when the South would rise again? Until a treasure hunter like Brewer finds definitive proof, we may never know. After all, the only people who *really* know are long dead.

In the end, one detail is unarguable: There will always be those searching for treasure. Never forget: We are a country founded on legends and myths. We love them, especially legends of treasure. Looking for treasure isn't just part of being an American, it is *America.*

I believe at least some of the rebel gold is still out there somewhere. But the bottom line is, the only reason the treasure's remained hidden for more than 150 years is because it was put there by experts. If it was easy to find, it would've been unearthed a long time ago. And as time marches on, the people with the necessary knowledge, like Bob Brewer, become fewer and farther between.

ABOVE
A PUBLIC HIDING PLACE
The first stop for the fleeing Confederates and their treasure may have been the last stop for a portion of the wealth. Some say that as much as $200,000 never left Danville, Virginia, and is buried in Green Hill Cemetery, still the focus of intense scrutiny by seekers of Confederate gold.

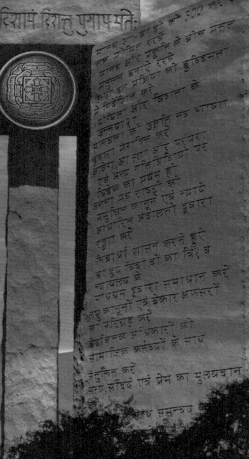

THE GEORGIA GUIDESTONES: AMERICA'S STONEHENGE

WHAT IF I TOLD YOU that America has its own Stonehenge? These giant stones were set up on a hillside outside, of all places, Atlanta in 1980. The man who had them built remains unknown, as does the monument's true purpose. In fact, other than their half-million-dollar price tag, almost nothing is known about the stones at all. They're composed of 119 tons of solid granite and have coded messages that are engraved into them in the world's eight most commonly spoken languages.

These rectangular pillars are also precisely crafted to track astrological and solar cycles. There are some who interpret the messages here as a sign of the end of days. Others theorize that they're a call for genocide on a massive scale. So what's the message they contain? Who built them? Why are they located on a remote hillside in Georgia? And, of course, what are they intended to guide us toward?

THE RAW NUMBERS

Take a look at the raw numbers to get a sense of how massive a project this was:

- Height: 19 feet 3 inches at its tallest point

- Height of the four basic stones: 16 feet 4 inches

- Weight: 237,746 pounds (about 119 tons)

- Capstone dimensions:

  - 9 feet 8 inches long

  - 6 feet 6 inches wide

  - 1 foot 7 inches thick

  - Weight: 24,832 pounds

- Total volume of granite used: 951 cubic feet

- Cost: $500,000

This was *not* a simple pile of rocks.

How and *why* the Guidestones were built have never been answered. But here's what we do know: The monument didn't just appear out of nowhere.

On a summer day in 1979, a man using the alias R. C. Christian shows up at the Elberton Granite Finishing Company, presents very detailed and specific plans, and tells them he wants to build the Georgia Guidestones. The only details we have about the man is that he was balding, with a fringe of white hair, and had an accent that suggested he was from one of the Plains states. Also, he had money—a lot of money. And the only thing he absolutely demanded was that he remain completely anonymous. To this day, no one has been able to figure out who he is.

What Christian commissioned, though, was no small undertaking. In fact, even with as deep a history of working with granite as Elberton had, they'd never encountered *anything* like the request from "R. C. Christian."

In fact, even if there was nothing more to the Georgia Guidestones than the stones themselves, the monument would be exceptionally impressive—a testament to the skills and abilities of the granite company R. C. Christian hired.

But there *is* more to the Guidestones than the granite slabs. Much more. Some say it's mysterious, others say it's sinister.

THE STONES

THE STONES WERE UNVEILED during a public ceremony in 1980. They were controversial immediately. Supporters like Yoko Ono

praised their message as a stirring call to rational thinking. But opponents attacked them, calling them the Ten Commandments of the Antichrist.

So what're the messages on the stones? First, you need to know that each message appears in English, Spanish, Swahili, Hindi, Hebrew, Arabic, Chinese, and Russian—the eight most widely spoken languages on Earth—which means the ten lines on each slab are intended for *all* of the world's inhabitants.

MAINTAIN HUMANITY UNDER 500 MILLION IN PERPETUAL BALANCE WITH NATURE.

But as for the messages themselves, the first nine, reading up from the bottom, seem to be a benign call to higher thinking: Don't be a cancer on the earth; seek harmony; balance personal rights with social duties; avoid petty laws; resolve international conflicts in a world court; protect people with fair laws; rule with reason; unite humanity with a new language; and guide reproduction wisely. But it's the topmost directive on the stones that stops everyone cold:

ORIENTATION TO THE STAR

In addition to the messages written on them, the Georgia Guide-stones are oriented to the stars:

- The east and west corners of the monument track sunrise and sunset.

- A slot cut in one of the slabs marks the winter and summer solstices.

- A shaft drilled through the central stone marks Polaris, the North Star.

- A slit cut through the capstone marks perfect noon.

SPANISH
CLASSICAL GREEK
SWAHILI
ENGLISH
EGYPTIAN HIEROGLYPHS
RUSSIAN
HINDI
HEBREW
ARABIC
CHINESE

Now reread that directive again.

A human population under 500 million would certainly be more "in balance" with nature. But . . .

To achieve a population under 500 million would mean that more than 7 billion of us would have to die.

Or be killed.

Now reread *that* again.

Exactly. The directive makes some believe that the Guidestones are calling for the mass murder of billions of innocent people—a global genocide that would kill the vast majority of the human race.

Which interpretation is accurate? Or is there another interpretation altogether?

The only way to find out is to decode who—or what—is behind the creation of the Guidestones themselves.

No question, whoever built the Georgia Guidestones, they were determined to protect their anonymity. So to find out more about the mysterious R. C. Christian, we began by talking to Guidestone historian Raymond Wiley, coauthor of *The Georgia Guidestones: America's Most Mysterious Monument.* According to Wiley, the pseudonym R. C. Christian is a clue itself—a fairly blatant one—that hearkens back to a 15-century physician and mystic named Christian Rosenkreutz, the idea of the Rose Cross, and the secretive organization known as the Rosicrucians.

THE ROSICRUCIANS

PEOPLE THINK THAT THE Freemasons are fascinating. Let me tell you about the Rosicrucians. Christian Rosenkreutz is said to have founded the secretive Rosicrucian

Society in Germany in the early 15th century, but some dispute that the man even lived at all. Some people say he's not even real. Others say he's more than one person.

For the members of the society, Rosenkreutz was a doctor who had spent a lifetime gathering what he called sacred knowledge. Studying ancient Turkish, Sufi, and Persian paths toward understanding, as well as Western medical knowledge, he supposedly traveled through the Middle East, being instructed by masters of ancient wisdom.

When he returned, Rosenkreutz supposedly founded his own church to pass on the learning to make sure that it didn't die with him. So, at first, all the members were doctors. Each one took an oath to heal the sick without payment, to maintain the secrecy of the fellowship, and to find a replacement for Rosenkreutz before he died.

The sacred knowledge is said to include elements of alchemy and psychic manipulation. Yup. Modern Rosicrucians are believed to have even been able to tap the ultimate power of the human mind. Some think the sect has evolved and they now seek to protect and guide humanity away from its own destruction. Others have accused the Rosicrucians of being out-and-out evil. To be clear, there are offshoots of Rosicrucians everywhere.

The symbol of the church was this: a cross with a white rose at its center. They call it a rosy cross. The *R* and the *C* from the words *Rosy Cross* undoubtedly represent the founder's last name—Rosenkreutz—and some believe they're a

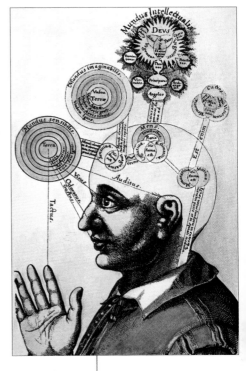

ABOVE

THE POWER OF THE MIND

Psychic manipulation and harnessing the powers of the human mind are at the heart of Rosicrucian sacred knowledge. This early-17th-century engraving shows human mental abilities classified in terms of God and the universe.

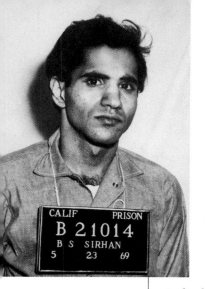

ABOVE
SIRHAN SIRHAN
Robert F. Kennedy's assassin was a Rosicrucian — by mail order. The idea that those beliefs played any part in his crime is considered ridiculous by most historians.

FACING PAGE TOP
SYMBOL OF ROSICRUCIANISM
A cross with a rose like this one at its center is exactly what the arrangement of the Georgia Guidestones resembles from above.

FACING PAGE BOTTOM
EXHIBIT 8A

link to the *R* and the *C* in the Guidestones benefactor's pseudonym — R. C. Christian.

And ready for this? If you look at the Georgia Guidestones from above, they resemble . . . a cross with a rose affixed.

So is that the grand answer? Do the Georgia Guidestones serve as a beacon to followers of an all-but-forgotten religion that's dedicated to unlocking hidden powers of the mind?

I can't say it's the craziest idea I ever heard. Ever join a fraternity or sorority? The appeal — and power — of secret knowledge is always tantalizing. Indeed, people join secret societies in order to be a part of something special . . . something that will set them apart from the rest of us.

But in the wrong hands, this desire for secret knowledge can lead to something far less attractive. Something that, according to journalist and Rosicrucian investigator Van Smith, might even be evil.

"THE GEORGIA GUIDESTONES were built explicitly to survive an apocalypse," Smith asserts. More important, he believes "this apocalypse is going to be man-made." In fact, with the commandment that the population be reduced to 500 million people — and that 7 billion of us are going to have to die — he says that when it comes to the Guidestones, "What it really is, is humanity's tombstone."

To prove his point, Smith insists that the Rosicrucians have a mastery of psychic abilities, including:

- Psychokinesis: the ability to move objects with your mind

- Astral projection: the ability to travel vast distances in time and space by projecting your thoughts

- The ability to control the minds of others

It's that last one—controlling the minds of others—that Smith says is the most potentially dangerous of all Rosicrucian abilities. Indeed, he believes it's already played a part in one of the most notorious of all American assassinations: the 1968 murder of Senator Robert F. Kennedy by Sirhan Sirhan.

That's right. Smith believes that Sirhan Sirhan assassinated Senator Kennedy not of his own volition, but under direct psychic guidance from secret Rosicrucian masters. His proof? The ramblings of Sirhan's diaries, and the fact that the killer was a Rosicrucian.

With all due respect to Smith, I've got to disagree. Sure, Sirhan Sirhan was technically a Rosicrucian, but he became one by mail order. Right. Mail order. I can be a *bride* by mail order, so to me, mail order doesn't quite count. And it doesn't seem as if Sirhan represented anybody or anything but himself. Look at the historical record. During Sirhan's trial, five different mental-health experts all testified that Sirhan was a paranoid schizophrenic. So the idea that the Rosicrucians were somehow controlling his mind, mentally manipulating him to shoot Senator Kennedy, well . . . that's just preposterous to me.

I will say it's worth looking at those mail-order ads. They appeared in the back pages of science fiction and hobbyist magazines in the 1950s and 1960s and even earlier (see Exhibit 8A, page 45). There, among the other odd advertisements, were some for a group calling themselves the Rosicrucians. The advertised mix of the promise of mysterious powers and the ability to unleash those powers for your own benefit was just the sort of nuttiness that could attract the applications, and the membership fees, of the foolish, the young and gullible . . . and even someone lonely and the criminally disturbed.

So how do you find the truth about Rosicrucians? We went to someone who would know, a Rosicrucian herself.

A REAL ROSICRUCIAN

THE VERY FIRST THING Reverend Bette Benner wanted you to know about Rosicrucianism was, "If someone tells you they're a Rosicrucian, they're not."

Wait a minute. This is a religion that's supposedly out to conquer the world, or at least win converts, and its *real* members won't tell you they're real members?

Not exactly, as Reverend Benner explained. True Rosicrucians perceive the belief as a quest, a pursuit, one that persists throughout one's life. "We identify ourselves as *students of the philosophy*," Reverend Benner told us.

This is important. Reverend Benner made it clear to us that Rosicrucians aspire to improvement, to growth, to the development of their spiritual and mental powers on an *individual basis*. And that the model for these pursuits and studies is none other than Jesus.

Therein, she pointed out, lies the great conflict between

well-established churches—and particularly the Roman Catholic Church—and the Rosicrucians.

If a church teaches that Jesus was divine, the Son of God, she observed, then that's that—we can follow such a figure, but we cannot aspire to become a figure like him.

But, the reverend said, if Jesus was a man, one who applied himself and developed his spirit and his mind to an almost unbelievable degree, that's something else altogether. We can all apply ourselves to developing our own skills and abilities, some of which, she believes, may be almost godlike in their reach and power. "We do believe in the powers of the mind. And we teach that 'As you believe, so shall it be unto you,'" she says, referring in a very different way to the possibility of advanced mental powers and capabilities.

What about using those powers to impose Rosicrucian will upon the world?

To Reverend Benner, that doesn't sound like true Rosicrucianism at all. "This is a very individualistic belief system," she says without hesitation. Imposing one individual's will upon another's—or upon billions of others—is the very antithesis of Rosicrucianism. "Imposing something goes way against our tradition of individual liberty," she said.

Reverend Benner didn't take Smith's Sirhan Sirhan conspiracy theories any more seriously than I did. And she offered an interesting take on whether or not the Rosicrucians

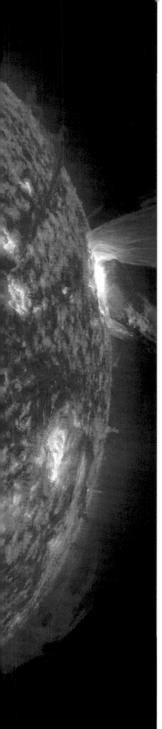

were behind the creation and construction of the Georgia Guidestones.

"Again," she said, "I think it's more likely that it's an individual who has studied our teachings and philosophy."

That, I find intriguing, and convincing. Far from being a secret mind-control cabal of the sort that Smith so deeply fears, Reverend Benner's portrait of Rosicrucianism is of a loosely connected group of seekers after higher truths. One of those seekers may have found his higher truth best expressed in the creation of the Georgia Guidestones.

Do I believe that those higher truths could include psychic abilities and other wild talents? Not necessarily. But the point is that rather than take the word of someone on the Internet who, bless him, starts out looking to *find* a conspiracy, and thus colors everything he sees with his own prejudgments, we actually sought out and spoke with someone who actively practices the beliefs in question. In talking with Reverend Benner, we not only learned quite a bit, we also gained some real insights into a possible motivation for the Georgia Guidestones.

That's the essence of decoding a mystery—going to the sources, and not being satisfied with secondhand reports. And that's the approach that brought us to a documentary filmmaker and Rosicrucian researcher who offered some of the most startling insights of all. The fact that they were insights that history has since disproved is another vital lesson in the process.

THE 2012 CONNECTION

AUTHOR AND FILMMAKER JAY WEIDNER flatly

"Rosicrucians are actively trying to warn us of the large threats our whole world faces. They are trying to set forth some rules so that people who survive the coming catastrophe can remake the world in a better way."

— JAY WEIDNER, AUTHOR AND FILMMAKER

states that the Rosicrucians not only aren't out to murder 7 billion of their fellow humans, they're actively trying to warn us of the large threats our whole world faces.

Particularly, Weidner told us in 2011, the threat was of a massive cycle of solar storms, possibly capable of disrupting or even destroying the global communications network and power grid . . . and bringing about the collapse of civilization.

Weidner's concerns regarding a 2012 solar storm cycle killing off most of us didn't come true, any more than the Mayan Calendar predictions of the end of the world did. 2012 was far from the best year this old planet has seen, but it was also far from the last year . . . or, as 2020 showed, even the worst.

But that wouldn't change the possibility that R. C. Christian, in 1979, might have believed that the coming cycle of solar storms was going to bring a dramatic end to the world as we know it, and do so around the year 2012.

For that matter, University of Georgia astronomer Loris Magnani pointed out to us that the peak current

FACING PAGE
SOLAR STORMS
The Guidestones' creator, R. C. Christian, may have believed that a coming cycle of solar storms was going to bring a dramatic end to the world.

cycle of solar explosions was due in 2012 or 2013. Not that he believed that even a catastrophic coronal mass ejection—a huge ball of energy cast out of the sun and, if the conditions are right, thrust onto a collision course with Earth—would bring an end to life as we know it.

Far likelier to do that, he argued, would be the impact of an asteroid on the earth. It was just such an impact—of an asteroid or a portion of a comet—that brought an end to the dinosaurs 65 million years or so ago.

At the same time, we live in such near-total dependence upon advanced technologies that even a minimal disruption of the power grid and communications networks would be catastrophic if not truly cataclysmic or apocalyptic. We've seen this in tragic miniature in the aftermath of a major storm such as Katrina or Sandy, the tsunami in Japan, fires in Australia, and devastating earthquakes and volcanoes.

Turn off the electricity, cut off the phones and the Internet. And—what?

We find out very quickly just how fragile the veneer of civilization is when you take away lights, refrigeration, air-conditioning, telephone, and all the rest. In the case of a major regional disaster such as a storm or earthquake, neighboring systems can step in and offer assistance. But take out the entire grid across the country—or the planet—and leave it off for more than a very few days, and you're going to have panic, breakdowns of order, looting, hoarding, possibly starvation, potentially a dramatic decrease in population.

Leave the lights off for a very few weeks and you have . . . a potential depopulation apocalypse.

And that, whatever the precise details and dates of such an apocalypse, is what Jay Weidner believes lies behind the Georgia Guidestones.

"They are trying to set forth some rules so that people who survive the coming catastrophe can remake the world in a better way," he said.

Far from being an evil, satanic group trying to destroy the world, the Rosicrucians (as Weidner understands them) are trying to *warn* us.

That makes sense to me — far more sense than trying to imagine a small group of people plotting the murder of 7 billion people.

But it still doesn't answer the question of who R. C. Christian is — or was.

MYSTERY BUILDER

THINK ABOUT THIS — if *you* had a vision of an American Stonehenge, a massive granite creation bearing your philosophy for the world, and you possessed the resources to underwrite its creation, would *you* want to keep your name out of it? For most of us, I think the answer would be "probably not." Our egos and our vanity might insist that we take at least some of the credit. Yet among the inscriptions on the monument is the announcement that their byline is a pseudonym. Is this humility — or deliberate misdirection?

Human nature and the role vanity plays in it would seem to rule out one name often mentioned as a possible source of funding for the Guidestones: Ted Turner, media mogul and one of America's largest individual owners of

BELOW
TED TURNER
The media mogul and America's largest individual owner of real estate has often been mentioned as a possible source of funding for the Guidestones. But, c'mon, can you really imagine the "Mouth of the South" not taking credit for this one?

real estate. At one point, Turner argued that the earth would be better served by a far smaller population than our present numbers, a statement that generated much controversy at the time. But while the ideas expressed on the stones, if interpreted benignly, do reflect Turner's well-known global harmony and environmental concerns, modesty, humility, and anonymity are not qualities often—or maybe ever— associated with the man once widely referred to as the "Mouth of the South."

So if the man behind the Georgia Guidestones wasn't Turner or, probably, any other high-profile, well-heeled philanthropist or visionary, who was he?

Only a few people ever met him. One was attorney Wyatt Martin, who handled the legal matters related to the Guidestones, and who signed a vow never to discuss his client, a vow he has kept.

Another was Hudson Cone, who was present at the granite company when the Guidestones were being created. Cone remembers Christian as a tall, balding man, with a fringe of white hair. He was well spoken and comported himself well. He gave no indication of who—or what—he represented.

That ambiguity, Cone believes to this day, was deliberate.

"Any time you have something with an air of mystery around it," he said, "you invite different interpretations."

Those differing interpretations, Cone insists, are one of the things that have kept the Georgia Guidestones at the center of so much speculation and public interest. He has had people tell him that the site is the holiest spot, while others argue that it's a profane location, a focal point for satanic power and ultimate evil.

Cone doesn't believe that the spot or the Guidestones are evil. In fact, he thinks that the *questions* the Guidestones raise are themselves its truest purpose.

"I believe it was put here to stimulate curiosity," Cone said.

That, too, makes a lot of sense to me. What better way to get people talking—and *thinking*—about the nature of our relationship to the world and to one another—than by creating an enormous mystery . . . and presenting that mystery in the world's great languages so that *all* can participate in the discussion?

After all, as Reverend Benner told us, the purpose of the Rosicrucians is to *pursue* higher knowledge, and one of the great and proven methods of pursuing knowledge is by provoking discussion.

What about those higher mental powers that the Rosicrucians seek? Is there anything to that? More than you might expect—as we discovered when we visited Dr. Melody Moore Jackson at the Georgia Institute of Technology.

As Dr. Jackson demonstrated—to our amazement— we are in a golden age of advancement in brain science, and particularly in our ability to control brain waves and enhance our ability to use our very thoughts to directly manipulate objects.

While Dr. Jackson, like most reputable scientists, doesn't place much faith in astral projection or some of the wilder speculations surrounding Rosicrucian mental powers, she does point out that our increasing ability to link brain waves to machines such as robotic

BELOW
THE UNVEILING
The Guidestones' unveiling in March 1980 was attended by more than 100 people. Once unveiled, the Stones immediately attracted controversy. Some said their messages called for a global embrace of rationalism and sustainability. Others said they were the Ten Commandments of the Antichrist.

arms, hands, and other prosthetics offers great promise to amputees and people who have paraplegia or quadriplegia.

What most intrigued us was her observation that only about 20 percent of those who attempt to use her equipment to guide their brain waves into direct contact and manipulation of objects do so on the first try.

That got us thinking. If two people out of ten have an innate ability to use their brain waves on a higher level than the rest of us—maybe there is something to the Rosicrucian belief that these abilities do exist, and can be developed.

WHY GEORGIA?

One question that has remained throughout our investigation of the Georgia Guidestones—why Georgia? Why were the stones placed on their particular site?

Turns out there's a serious—and mysterious—reason for that as well.

The theory of Earth Changes, first propounded by the mystic Edgar Cayce early in the 20th century, argues that we are rapidly approaching a time of devastating changes to the surface of the earth. Those changes could be the result of earthquakes, asteroid or comet impact, super volcanoes, solar flares—whatever. As we've seen, particularly in terms of the 2012 believers—but also as with previous apocalypse believers such as those who feared the end of the world would accompany the new millennium, or those who saw global devastation coming as Halley's Comet returned, or any of the hundreds of other doomsday faiths that have come and gone—the specific details of the actual apocalypse vary from believer to believer, and some of them have already been proven inaccurate.

What matters for the purposes of decoding the Guidestones is the *consequences* of the devastation.

And those consequences include a radically altered surface of the earth—a surface that will lack many of the most familiar features of the world we know.

What sort of features?

Minor things like: California, New York City, parts of Florida, and other landmasses throughout the world.

That's scary.

But according to Cayce's Earth Changes theory, it turns out that in addition to the changes that would alter the physical face of the world, there are "safe zones" that would ride out the earth changes, and in doing so provide a psychic focus for the energies needed to rebuild the world.

Where are those safe zones?

You guessed it—one of them is in rural Georgia. (See Exhibit 8B, page 56, for a map.)

It's where the Guidestones stand, meaning they're ready to help the survivors of the earth changes rebuild the world. And rebuild it *better.*

I believe that the Georgia Guidestones are, on one level, exactly what they appear to be—a tool for getting people to think about the nature of existence, and the ways in which that existence could be improved.

I think that there's a good chance that the person behind them was a Rosicrucian.

But I also think that there's a motivation for the stones

FACING PAGE TOP & BOTTOM
EARTH CHANGES
According to the Earth Changes theory, the Georgia Guidestones are located in a zone that's safe from devastating changes to the earth's surface: earthquakes, floods, asteroids, volcanoes, solar flares—disasters that some believe will bring an end to modern civilization.

SAFE ZONES MAP
of the United States of America

Spokane

Denver

Chicago

Washington, D.C.

Kansas City

Phoenix

Georgia Guidestones

Dallas

Orlando

LEGEND

☐ SAFE ZONE   ● TROUBLE ZONE

Earth changes—earthquakes, floods, solar flares—may cause massive changes to the land masses all around the world. Should this occur, the areas shown in purple may be under the sea.

ABOVE
EXHIBIT 8B

that may have been overlooked, and that the motivation lies in the times during which they were commissioned and created.

The Georgia Guidestones came into being in the late 1970s and early 1980s—a time of enormous international tension between the United States and the then-existing Soviet Union. At the heart of those tensions: tens of thousands of nuclear warheads, an arsenal of destruction aimed at each other's throats and more than capable of bringing civilization down in a mass of radioactive rubble.

They were among the scariest times in human history—and a reminder that we don't need an apocalypse beyond our control to end the world. For more than half a century, we have held the power to do it ourselves. Self-inflicted genocide by nuclear bombs controlled by our governments: No secret cabals need apply.

And I think that it was the possibility of just such a nuclear holocaust that prompted R. C. Christian to create the message he placed on the Georgia Guidestones. A message intended for the survivors of a global nuclear holocaust. A message designed to help them restore a balance to the earth — and to avoid the mistakes that destroyed their ancestors.

That, I think, is the purpose of the Georgia Guidestones, and that's the message we decoded during our investigation.

Of course, there's one person, if he's still alive, who knows whether or not my interpretation is accurate, and that's R. C. Christian, but he's not talking.

I just hope that he does come forth, and tell us whether or not any of our interpretations of the Georgia Guidestones are accurate. Or if there is another interpretation — perhaps brighter, perhaps darker — that we may have overlooked.

Until then, we have the Georgia Guidestones themselves, speaking their message to the ages — and to each of us in their own way.

WHERE IS DB COOPER !?

DB COOPER:
AMERICAN OUTLAW

WHAT IF I TOLD YOU that of all of America's skyjackings, only one remains unsolved?

On November 24, 1971, a passenger using the name Dan Cooper hijacked Northwest Orient Airlines Flight 305, headed from Portland to Seattle (see Exhibit 7A, page 61, the hijacker's ticket voucher). After threatening to blow up the plane with a bomb, Cooper demanded four parachutes and $200,000.

Fearing the worst, Northwest Airlines agreed. Once on the ground in Seattle, Cooper let the other passengers and some of the flight crew off the plane and had the money and parachutes brought on board. The plane refueled, took off again, and, at 10,000 feet, Cooper jumped from the back stairs of the Boeing 727 into the Pacific Northwest night.

He was never seen again.

The press began call-
ing the skyjacker *DB Cooper,*
and the FBI investigated
thousands of leads. Suspects
included a mass murderer,
a college professor, a career
criminal, and a World War II
veteran. But they were all ruled out as the culprit. In the
last 40 years, new suspects have emerged, and now we
have an unexamined lead that may point to an inside job.
We need to decode who he was and how he may have
managed to pull off this unbelievable stunt without ever
getting caught.

Whatever the case, I can tell you one thing: When
someone commits the perfect crime, I want to know who
he is.

TO THIS DAY, it's one of America's greatest unsolved rob-
beries. But Robert Blevins's book *Into the Blast* presents a
promising lead.

Kenneth Peter Christiansen, a former Northwest
Airlines employee, was never really a formal suspect in
the DB Cooper case. But thanks to *Into the Blast*, Kenny
Christiansen has come to the forefront of possible suspects. We got Blevins to talk with us, and I have to admit,
he makes a compelling case.

"I would say I'm ninety percent to ninety-five percent
certain Christiansen was DB Cooper," Blevins asserted.
"He worked for the airline. He had paratrooper training. He had the opportunity. He had a lot of unexplained
spending within a few months after the hijacking. He lent
his best friend's sister five thousand dollars in cash to buy

a house. Then he used another sixteen thousand dollars to buy another house for himself. As far as we can tell, Kenny Christiansen had one life before the hijacking and a completely different one afterward."

When you look at the numbers, you definitely start smelling something fishy. While working for Northwest Airlines, Christiansen never earned more than $512 a month—*that's a month*—which even in the early 1970s didn't go far. Yet within a few months of the skyjacking, he suddenly had a stash of money to throw around.

So why didn't the FBI take a harder look at Christiansen as a suspect?

Blevins chalks the oversight up to three preconceptions the FBI brought to the case:

1. Christiansen didn't match eyewitness descriptions of the skyjacker.
2. He had no previous criminal history.
3. The FBI didn't believe that the skyjacker had military training or background.

BELOW
EXHIBIT 7A
Airline ticket voucher

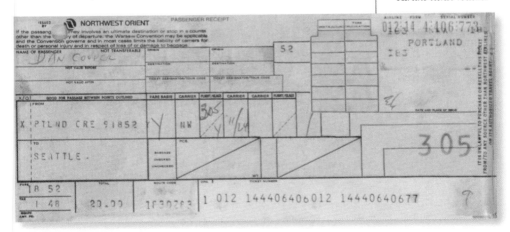

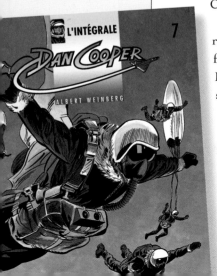

L'INTÉGRALE   7

Dan Cooper

ALBERT WEINBERG

Let's look at this piece by piece, starting with what, to me, is the most glaring question: Why would they think that DB Cooper had no military training?

According to Blevins: "The parachute that DB Cooper actually jumped with is called a Navy Backpack Six, and it's a smaller parachute, more of a military type. The skyjacker was a pretty tough guy." Blevins added, "Kenny went through paratrooper training where they started out with two hundred and sixty-two men and ended up with eighty that actually finished, and he was one of them."

All of these factors have convinced Blevins that he's cracked the DB Cooper case. He has few doubts that Christiansen is the culprit.

"I think he jumped out of the back of that 727, hit the ground, popped off his parachute, disconnected the harness and the container from it, buried the silk part, and put his briefcase and the money bag into the container for the parachute, put it on his back, and walked out of the woods."

At first look, though, Blevins's case is mostly circumstantial, which means we need to look at other pieces of evidence—and circumstances—to tell us whether Kenny Christiansen was really DB Cooper.

The trail to investigate whether DB Cooper really was the late Kenny Christiansen had led us from writer Robert Blevins to Kenny's brother, Lyle, who dropped an amazing bombshell when we spoke with him.

"Before he passed away," Lyle says of his brother, Kenny, who died in 1994, "he told me on his deathbed, 'There's something you should know, but I cannot tell you.'"

And that's the part where my spider-sense started to tingle. You know how they say don't believe everything you hear? There's only one exception to that: a deathbed confession. It is the only reason I'm so obsessed with this case—and with Kenny Christiansen. After his near-confession, Lyle spent years thinking about Kenny's life—and decided he needed to examine his brother's possessions way more carefully.

The first thing he found?

According to Lyle, on that fateful day, "the skyjacker came on the airline with an attaché case. And I found this very same attaché case in Kenny's final effects."

OK. They both have briefcases. So did my dad. That doesn't mean I'm related to DB Cooper.

Then Lyle started looking at the composite sketch that law enforcement put together. The descriptions of DB Cooper when he boarded the flight were all the same. He was wearing a black suit with a tie and carrying a briefcase. He was described as tall and dark-haired. Look at Exhibit 7B (page 65), the FBI bulletin featuring a sketch based on eyewitness reports.

And then Lyle showed us the photo on page 64:

"I found this picture in his photo book. I must have looked at the photo book many times and never caught it, and one day I said, 'Wait a minute.' Carrying a bag, looks like a bag of money, and he's got the attaché case."

Again, does that make him guilty? Not by a long shot. In fact, the Dan Cooper who boarded that flight—wearing a black suit and tie and carrying a briefcase—was described by eyewitnesses as having dark hair, being in his 40s, and standing 5 feet 10 inches to 6 feet tall.

Kenny Christiansen was bald and stood 5 feet 8 inches, so the physical description doesn't match. But we all know

BOMBS ON PLANES

Such a scenario is all but unimaginable today. But you have to remember that this was the early 1970s, and airline security was nothing like it is now. There were no ID checks before boarding a plane. You could still smoke on planes. It was like Studio 54 up there.

After the DB Cooper sky-jacking, things began to change. Boeing installed something called the "Cooper vane" on the rear doors of all 727s, making it impossible to lower those doors from inside the airplane. The FAA also began installing metal detectors in airports to screen passengers and their carry-on luggage.

FACING PAGE

A COMIC ALIAS
Some say the hijacker took the name "Dan Cooper" from a Franco-Belgian comic series about a fictional Canadian military flying ace and rocket ship pilot.

BELOW

IN THE BAG

Kenny Christiansen's brother, Lyle, found this photo of Kenny—carrying a briefcase and what looks like a bag of money—tucked behind another in a family album. Why was the photo hidden? And why was it kept?

that eyewitness accounts are fairly unreliable. They're dubious at best. And the other thing we know: Lyle said that Kenny used to wear a toupee *prior* to the skyjacking, but he never wore it again *after* the skyjacking. Again, great circumstantial evidence, for sure. But we need something that's far more concrete.

So let's look at some other pieces of the puzzle:

- The skyjacker was left-handed—and so was Kenny.
- On the plane, the skyjacker ordered bourbon—Kenny Christiansen's preferred drink.
- The skyjacker smoked—and so did Kenny.

KENNY'S MONEY

BUT PERHAPS MOST INTERESTING of all was the photo that Lyle showed us: of Kenny Christiansen carrying a briefcase and what looks like a paper bag of money. At first, just seems like any other old photo, right? But in this case, the picture had been in Kenny Christiansen's photo album—*hidden behind a different, more innocuous photo.*

Just darn creepy, right? Hiding the photo of yourself walking in with your big bag of money? Sure, it makes me raise an eyebrow, but even assuming all this is true, when you look at the case, it's still missing the most important thing of all: motive.

What would cause someone who had been, by all accounts, a quiet man who caused little trouble to suddenly pull off the biggest unsolved crime in American aviation history? And why mount that crime against his own employer?

Turns out there's an explanation for that, too—one that's found in Kenny Christiansen's own handwriting. According to his letters, Kenny was never able to earn a stable living at Northwest because of constant protracted labor disputes at his job. There were eight strikes at Northwest Airlines between 1954 and 1971, and those strikes severely cut into his earning power. He was constantly having to take odd jobs like working in a hotel or digging ditches for friends just to make ends meet.

That is not a euphemism. Kenny Christiansen was actually *digging ditches.*

ABOVE
EXHIBIT 7B
FBI bulletin

In the meantime, the $8 million jets that he worked on sat unused on the ground, and make no mistake, this hardworking former paratrooper resented it. If we believe that Kenny Christiansen was DB Cooper, then by 1971, he had simply had enough and decided to strike out at the airline to make them pay for the struggles they'd put him through.

Right there, we get our first taste of an actual motive. But y'know what convinces me even more than that?

Kenny Christiansen's bank statements.

The question of whether or not DB Cooper survived the jump is essential. Former FBI agent Ralph Himmelsbach told us that he thought it was highly unlikely.

But in April 1972, a man named Richard McCoy skyjacked a United Airlines 727 and demanded half a million dollars.

McCoy jumped at 16,000 feet while the plane was traveling at 200 miles per hour. And he survived.

The similarities to the Cooper case were such that authorities thought for a while that McCoy *was* DB Cooper. But McCoy didn't resemble the descriptions of Cooper at all, and it turned out that he had been home having Thanksgiving dinner in Utah when Cooper pulled off his caper.

For me, though, the point is that if McCoy could survive a jump from 6,000 feet *higher* than Cooper, there's no way to just dismiss Cooper's jump and say it's unlikely he survived.

At the time of his death, this man who used to dig actual ditches had $186,000 socked away in savings, and over $20,000 in his checking account. Add that to the sums he spent so freely in the months after the skyjacking, and you get another big piece of the puzzle, this one with dollar signs all over it.

Still, even with the motive and the overflowing bank account, it doesn't mean he absolutely was DB Cooper. But when you stack all the pieces together, you do have to wonder, *Could it all be coincidence?* And even more than that, *Why wasn't this paratrooper one of the FBI's suspects?*

THE FBI'S SIDE OF THE STORY

OF COURSE, WE APPROACHED the FBI. They told us that the DB Cooper case was never solved and, as a result, it's still an open investigation.

We did, however, get something that may be even better: Ralph Himmelsbach, the retired FBI agent who was actually in charge of the Cooper investigation from 1971 to 1980. Himmelsbach described the night of the skyjacking as stormy, windy, rainy—a lousy night for flying at all, much less for jumping out of a jet airplane.

To help us reconstruct the crime and understand how the FBI saw it, Himmelsbach arranged for us to accompany him onto a Boeing 727—in 1971, the most widely flown airliner in the world.

Dan Cooper (he wouldn't become DB until a news story assigned the initials to him in the days after the skyjacking) was in seat 18C. As a flight attendant approached him, he handed her a note.

"You better read this, miss. I have a bomb," the passenger in 18C said to her.

"He told her to take that note up to the cockpit, and his instruction to them was to stay in the air until they got to Seattle while the money and the parachutes were obtained," Himmelsbach explained. "If they did anything wrong, he would set off the bomb."

At this point, we know where DB Cooper was sitting; we know about the note and the demands it made. When the FBI asked the airline how they wanted to deal with the hijacker, the head of the airline was determined to keep everyone safe. The airline agreed to pay the ransom and handed over the four parachutes the hijacker requested. At that point, the hijacker selected an older-style military parachute of the sort that Kenny Christiansen might've been familiar with. Then he opened the rear door of the 727 and, at 10,000 feet, jumped out.

Beyond that, there's nothing.

Former agent Himmelsbach thinks there's a very good reason for that.

He doesn't think Cooper survived the jump.

"I can't say that it wasn't survivable," he observed. "But it's unlikely. That airliner was going one hundred and seventy knots at ten thousand feet. Outside air temperature is seven degrees below zero, with a chill factor of about sixty-nine degrees below zero."

It's a strong point, right? But it doesn't answer the most important question—the question people have been asking for four decades:

If Cooper didn't survive the jump, why was no trace ever found of his body?

"The best explanation I can give you of that is just go look at those woods," the former lead investigator replied.

And that's the FBI's explanation. DB Cooper died in the jump, his body was claimed by some animal in the woods, and his clothing, parachute, and all the money were lost to time and the elements. As for why they don't think he was a Northwest Airlines employee? They say he would've been recognized.

Both of those are certainly explanations. They're just not explanations I buy.

Hijacker remains at large

Where's D.B. Cooper? Journal Reward Aids Search

Have you seen 'D. B. Cooper'?

The man calling himself "D. B. Cooper" who hijacked a Northwest 727 and extorted $200,000 in the process last November is the subject of a widespread manhunt. During the episode, "Cooper" demonstrated more than a passing knowledge of the air environment, especially parachuting. He also showed a fair familiarity with airline aircraft operation.

It is possible that "D. B. Cooper's" path may have crossed that of airline personnel at some time under another name. He expressed a bitter hatred for the airlines and may have worked for one.

From descriptions furnished by

Height: 5 feet 10 inches to 6 feet
Weight: 170 to 180 pounds
Build: Average to well built
Complexion: Olive, Latin appearance, medium smooth
Hair: Dark brown or black, normal style, parted on left, combed back sideburns, low ear level
Eyes: Possibly brown; during latter part of flight put on dark wrap-around sunglasses with dark rim
Voice: Low, spoke intelligently, no particular accent
Characteristic: Heavy smoker of Raleigh filter-tip cigarettes
Wearing apparel: Black suit, white shirt, narrow black tie, black dress suit, black rain-type overcoat or dark topcoat, brown shoes; carried paper bag 4 inches by 12 inches

The FBI is still looking for him and money. The Journal is offering $1,000 for first $20 of that money to be turned in. If 10,000 bills that serial numbers of any of money matches serial numbers of any of serial numbers are to be found or

Let me say this: I have great respect for the FBI. But I think the FBI underestimated just how smart a guy DB Cooper was—and just how carefully he prepared his heist.

- He insisted that the pilot stay below 10,000 feet; any higher and they'd have to pressurize the cabin, making it even harder for Cooper to open the plane's rear door and escape.

- He also asked that the flaps—y'know know those things on the wings that go up and down at takeoff and landing . . . ? He asked that those be set at *exactly* 15 degrees. Why? At that angle, the 727 couldn't fly any faster than 200 mph, making it safer for Cooper to jump out.

However you slice it, this guy knew what he was doing. He knew about planes, he knew how they worked, and he certainly used that knowledge to his advantage. Of course, I'm no expert on jumping from a jet aircraft. So we turned to someone who is.

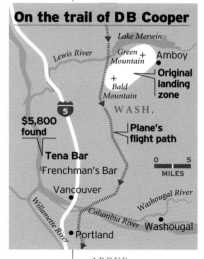

On the trail of DB Cooper

ABOVE
POINTS ON THE MAP
Almost nine years after the hijacking—and 40 miles from Cooper's supposed landing point—an eight-year-old boy found $5,800 in bills that matched the serial numbers of Cooper's take.

COULD HE HAVE SURVIVED?

LARRY YOUNT IS A PARACHUTE EXPERT with more than 200 military jumps and more than 4,000 civilian skydives.

While he's never jumped from a plane moving at 200 mph (civilian skydives are generally made from planes traveling at about 90 mph), he's made military jumps from aircraft that are traveling at speeds up to 150 mph.

SCOTT: The "eureka" moment came after Buddy shoved me through the small opening in the roof that led to Kenny Christiansen's attic. None of us, Brad included, believed we'd find anything this many years after Kenny had lived there. The only thing I noticed was some insulation had been moved around slightly. I could barely see it with my flashlight. Without really thinking about it, I sort of shoved the insulation back into place.

That's when I felt the top of a trapdoor of a hiding place that may indeed have hidden DB Cooper's ill-gotten loot. My heart trembled as I opened the lid. While the hiding place was empty, I have no doubt that someone had made a small hiding place in that attic that was almost impossible to find. And the house was owned by a guy who was a trained paratrooper, worked for Northwest Orient Airlines, drank bourbon and smoked Raleighs (just like Cooper did), bought the house with cash, and apparently left a bundle of $20 bills hidden outside that were found by some kids years later.

I've tried weaker cases and won them . . .

So we asked him flat-out: When DB Cooper leaped from the plane, he had a bag of money weighing 22 pounds tied to his waist. Is that too much weight?

Yount didn't think so. "Twenty-two pounds—it's almost inconsequential," he said, explaining that he's personally done military jumps with 150 pounds of equipment.

Taking it a step further, we asked Yount, if we re-created the conditions, would he be willing to jump out of a 727 at 200 mph and at 10,000 feet? Naturally, Yount said yes. But then he added something that floored us: "There are actually 727s in private fleets that are used for commercial skydiving. People pay extra money to go do the jump that DB Cooper did."

Read that again.

Not only are regular thrill-seekers *surviving* the Cooper jump—but they're making it a *regular practice.*

Gives new light to the FBI's assertion that Cooper died that night, doesn't it?

BEYOND MAKING THE ASSUMPTION that Cooper died, the FBI's other argument against Christiansen is based on the belief that he would've been known to the crew on Flight 305 as a Northwest Airlines employee.

It's an interesting hypothesis—until you realize that Flight 305 was a *domestic* flight—and much of Christiansen's experience was with *international* routes. Back then, there was not a lot of intermingling between domestic and overseas crews. So yes,

Even after Christiansen began throwing money around in the wake of the skyjacking, he continued to work for Northwest Airlines — and did so for 20 years. You've heard the cliché: The criminal always returns to the scene of the crime. If Kenny Christiansen was DB Cooper, he not only returned to the scene. He collected a paycheck from them for close to two decades.

if Kenny Christiansen *was* DB Cooper, he was certainly taking some risk that he could be recognized as a Northwest employee. But as he did with the plane's airspeed and altitude, it was a risk that could certainly be minimized.

At this point, we have plenty of circumstantial evidence that points to Christiansen. But if we really hope to decode the mystery, we need *hard* evidence.

And in the case of DB Cooper, hard evidence most likely means money.

On that night of the hijacking, DB Cooper asked for $200,000 in $20 bills, which he received. In total, that meant he was carrying 10,000 bills, divided into 100 bundles, for a total package that weighed about 22 pounds.

Yet before the money was delivered, the FBI was smart. They ran the bills through a Recordak machine that took a microfilm photograph of each bill, including the serial numbers. A few months after the skyjacking, the FBI published the serial numbers, a 34-page list that showed

A KID AND HIS MONEY

In 2008, the lucky eight-year-old boy who found the money was a grown man in his 30s. Forever a capitalist, he put some of the DB Cooper money up for auction in a Dallas auction house. And here's the kicker. The bidding for the most complete bill started at $750. Know what it finally sold for? $6,572.50!

And *that's* how you put a price on a piece of American history.

TOP
**DIGGING FOR
DOLLARS** . . .
*FBI agents dig alongside
the Columbia River
where $5,800 in badly
decomposed bills were
found in 1980. The serial
numbers matched those
that Cooper was given.*

BOTTOM
**. . . AND DREDGING
FOR DB**
*After the discovery of
part of Cooper's cash,
boaters dredged the
Columbia hoping to find
Cooper's body — to no
avail.*

people what to be on the alert for when a $20 bill crossed your desk. None of the bills ever showed up. . . .

That is, until February 1980, when the luckiest eight-year-old boy in the world found a bundle of waterlogged and decomposing $20 bills on the banks of the Columbia River near Vancouver, Washington. And that spot? It's about 40 miles from what authorities believe would have been DB Cooper's landing zone. There was $5,800 in 20s, and their serial numbers matched the FBI list.

As far as we know, this is the only confirmed incident of any of the DB Cooper money turning up.

STILL, even if Kenny Christiansen did pull off the skyjacking . . . even if he lost $5,800 of the ransom money during his escape . . . he'd *still* have had a *lot* of bills to stash. And because the serial numbers were so well known, he couldn't exactly take the bundles of cash to the nearest bank.

So if you had a ton of money sitting around and you wanted to keep it safe, where would you put it? You'd need a good hiding spot.

Which led us to the house that Christiansen bought in Washington State not long after the skyjacking.

TODAY, THE HOUSE Christiansen bought has been converted to a print shop. But according to the current owner, Dan Rattenbury, the printing company isn't the first commercial business to be located in the converted house, which was sold a dozen or so years ago.

So had any money been found on the property?

"I haven't," Rattenbury said. "But people have . . ."

Wait. *What?*

"People have found money on the property," he explained. "When the owner I bought it from bulldozed all the trees around here, they unknowingly unearthed some kind of plastic bag, they said, that was ripped open from being dragged through the stumps, probably. Kids were playing in the stumps, and they found a bag, and it had money in it."

Can we stop right there? On the property that used to belong to Kenny Christiansen, when they bulldozed the trees, they unearthed bags with money in it. And yes, I'm thinking what you're thinking: It's just local urban myth.

But it was also enough to make me bring in a modern infrared specialist who can scan the house and tell us if there's anything else hidden in Christiansen's old walls.

And that's where things got *truly* interesting.

THROUGHOUT THIS BOOK, we're trying to show you exactly what it was like to participate in our historical investigations. But let me give you one additional detail: On the night when the *Decoded* team was scanning Kenny Christiansen's old house with infrared, they were on the West Coast. I was on the phone on the East Coast.

Seeing it was getting late, the director said to me, "Brad, we don't need you anymore. We probably won't find anything."

And I think, *We probably won't find anything.* So I hang up, intent on enjoying my night.

Then my phone rang. It was the director. I could hear his voice shaking.

"Brad . . . I think we found something."

WE FOUND SOMETHING

AT THE BACK OF THE COPY SHOP, the team was running a thermal scan on the walls and ceiling of what used to be Kenny Christiansen's bedroom. In most spots, the thermal image reads red, showing normal insulation. To our surprise, though, the scan suddenly went blue, turning up one interesting spot directly above the bedroom—a spot where the insulation appeared to be far less thick than in the rest of the ceiling.

Craning his neck upward, *Decoded* team member Scott Rolle didn't think much of it. It was probably just a break in the insulation. So he volunteered to go into the attic and investigate.

What happened next was unique in the *Decoded* experience. I give you Rolle, in his own words as he was crawling through the attic:

"All right, there's a lot of insulation . . . [there] definitely is some stuff pushed aside. Let me try to get closer. Hang on. . . ."

Rolle starts pushing some of the insulation aside.

"Right where we saw the infrared, it looks like something was there. I'm gonna try to move some of it around a little more. I don't see any money, but let me try to get in here further. Whoa!

"It's hard to describe, but it's . . . it's like you can lift up the flooring . . . yet . . . Oh my God. Wow. Holy cow. There is a—I just lifted up a piece of the floor, and there is a little space down here where something absolutely could have been. It's almost like it's a little hiding space, and it's—it's actually

right above the bedroom where Kenny Christiansen slept.

"Even though there's nothing here now, it would have been an excellent hiding place for money."

OK, let's hit the PAUSE button here. Look at the photo on the facing page with the insulation. Now look below it. See that?

That's a hiding spot. We found a hiding spot.

So unless you have secret trapdoors above *your* bedroom, there certainly doesn't seem to be anything accidental about it.

OK, TIME TO RECAP. So far, it seems that Christiansen had both the motive and the means to commit the crime. And in checking out the house he used to live in, we found a suspicious hiding place—a hinged cubbyhole in the ceiling above his bedroom. There's also that local legend about money being found in a plastic bag in the woods behind his house.

It all seems to be coming together—but there's one more aspect to the case worth pursuing, and it's a name found frequently in Kenny Christiansen's letters: Bernie Geestman.

Everyone knows a guy named Bernie, right?

But this name—*Bernie Geestman*—is all over the letters Kenny Christiansen wrote to his family. Obviously, he was somebody important to Christiansen—but was there a chance that Geestman could also have been important to DB Cooper?

Robert Blevins thinks so. In fact, he goes so far as to accuse Geestman of being Christiansen's accomplice. What would an accomplice have done? Blevins offers a detailed scenario:

ABOVE

KENNY'S HOUSE
In October 1972, about a year after Cooper's jump, Kenny Christiansen paid $14,000 for a modest ranch in Bonney Lake, a small mountain town in the Cascade Mountains of Washington State.

"He probably drove Cooper down to the Portland International Airport, dropped him off to catch the flight to Seattle, and then drove back up by himself to Paradise Point State Park. It's right next to the freeway in Battle Ground, less than two miles from where they found the money in 1980," Blevins insisted.

So Geestman was the one who helped Christiansen escape?

According to Blevins, Bernie "just waited for Kenny, and Kenny jumped out, hiked out—back out to the freeway, and they met up. It's only about a maybe twelve-, thirteen-mile walk, at the most, back to the freeway. And it's not a big wilderness like everybody thinks down there."

Sounds somewhat convincing, don't you think? But let me make this *very* clear: However convincing Blevins *sounds*, his theory is really just one man's opinion. So how do we find the truth? We went directly to Bernie Geestman and asked for *his* side of the story.

BERNIE AND KENNY

BERNIE GEESTMAN AND KENNY Christiansen knew each other for a long time. They worked side by side at the airline, refueling planes until Kenny moved to a job as a purser on Northwest's Tokyo flight. At one point Kenny Christiansen was renting a room from Bernie and his wife. Kenny attended Bernie's wedding. These guys played cards together. Bernie and Kenny were close friends for almost 40 years. Still, Bernie Geestman has a reputation for being tight-lipped. He's avoided talking about Kenny Christiansen for a long time now. But to our own surprise, he agreed to speak with us.

DECODED: Would you characterize Kenny Christiansen as a very, very good friend of yours?

GEESTMAN: Well, we were . . . You know, I-I wouldn't, uh . . . He was a friend of mine working together.

DECODED: From what we saw, you were dear friends prior to this. He had worked on your property. He was at your wedding. He was a good friend you had worked with.

GEESTMAN: He . . . I saw him.

DECODED: And at . . . at one point, you guys were good enough friends for Kenny to rent a room from you. He paid like fifty bucks a week or a month or something?

GEESTMAN: I never rented Kenny my room.

DECODED: Strange, because Kenny wrote letters to his family indicating that he was renting from you and paid fifty dollars a month.

GEESTMAN: He paid it to my wife, Margaret Ann Miller, at the time, and she was supposed to be taking care of the house while I was at sea.

DECODED: You must know that the reason we are really interested in Kenny Christiansen is that we're wondering if he is DB Cooper.

GEESTMAN: You're asking me my opinion?

DECODED: I am, yeah. Yes.

GEESTMAN: Yes. He looks exactly like the picture the FBI put out.

BELOW
**A POSSIBLE
ACCOMPLICE**
*Kenny Christiansen's
friend Bernie Geestman
(seen here with
Christiansen, right,
on Geestman's 1968
wedding day) is believed
by some to have aided
and abetted in the
hijacking.*

DECODED: So, you were suspicious right away, Bernie? That looked like Kenny to you?

GEESTMAN: Yes. I saw Kenny dying in his house. Would you say to your friend, "Now, Kenny, were you DB Cooper?"

It's an amazing question, right? Think about it a moment. Geestman's watching his friend on his deathbed, still wondering if he's really DB Cooper. We reminded him that the statute of limitations had run. He couldn't be prosecuted for this crime.

We reminded Geestman that he purchased an Airstream trailer around the time of the hijacking, then disappeared with it for several days around Thanksgiving. There was no explanation for where the trailer went. It suddenly just disappeared. We pointed out that he had knowledge of how these airplanes worked. And that Geestman happened to live in the area of the landing zone. And that Robert Blevins insisted that Bernie Geestman was Kenny Christiansen/DB Cooper's accomplice. But Geestman kept insisting one thing: "He's lying. . . . *I didn't do it. I never—I never, never was an accomplice to Kenny Peter Christiansen or anybody else.*"

And y'know what? Our *Decoded* team believed him.

This is the hardest part of playing *Charlie's Angels*. I wasn't in the room with the team. So I still have a hard time deciding what I think about Bernie. There's a part of me that feels like he's hiding something, but my *Decoded* team—Buddy Levy, Christine McKinley, and Scott Rolle—seem convinced he's not. These are my partners. I have to trust their instinct here. And yes, since our investigation, dozens of people have written emails asking us to look at Geestman's wife, Margaret Ann Miller. But in the end, though the team is done with Bernie Geestman, they still believe DB Cooper was Kenny Christiansen.

CONCLUSION

SO WHAT HAPPENS NOW? Only time will tell. Just recently, someone stepped forward saying that one of their relatives was DB Cooper. The FBI disagreed, which means, inevitably, someone else will be stepping forward in the near future. Now you can look at the evidence against Kenny Christiansen for yourself.

No question, Christiansen had both the motive and the means to pull off the skyjacking—and everyone in his circle seems to think he might've done it, too. Based on the evidence that we've shown you, you can see why Christiansen did it, how he did it, even how he spent his ransom money. But let's be clear about one thing: Though most people consider the DB Cooper skyjacking to have been a victimless crime, it wasn't. Ask the FBI and Northwest Airlines. Some say no one was hurt by what he did—that he's some kind of modern-day Robin Hood. That's why DB Cooper has become a folk hero. There were songs written about this guy, movies made about him. There's even a bar that celebrates the anniversary of the heist with a DB Cooper look-alike contest.

That may make you a celebrity, but that doesn't make you a hero.

ABOVE
UNCANNY
RESEMBLANCE
Photo of Kenny Christiansen without his usual toupee and police sketch of DB Cooper.

1826
East Room

AREA

·MAIN·FLOOR·PLAN·
PRESENT
·EXECUTIVE·MANSION·
James Hoban. Original Architect. 1792

Porte
1829

Cochere

AREA

Drawn by, Fred.D.Owen
Washington,.D.
Copyrighted. 1

·SECOND·STORY·
·PLAN·

THE WHITE HOUSE: WHERE IS THE CORNERSTONE OF DEMOCRACY?

WHAT IF I TOLD YOU that the cornerstone of our democracy is actually *missing*?

In 1792, stonemasons laid the cornerstone for the White House. It was the first piece in the most important government building in Washington, DC.

To this day, descriptions of the stone vary, from something small that you can carry . . . to something that's massive. The men who placed it were brothers in one of the world's most secretive organizations—of course, the Freemasons. The day after they put it down, the stone vanished. This thing just disappeared.

Some say it's been stolen. Others say it's missing or just misplaced. And the rumors about the stone itself are even wilder. In some descriptions, the stone was inscribed by our Founding Fathers.

In others, it's hollow, containing landmark documents of great, unimagined wisdom. Many believe the stone was stolen by the Masons themselves. But the Masons, of course, deny any involvement.

Whatever the case, for more than 200 years now, the location of this cornerstone—the very first piece of the White House—has been a mystery. Indeed, everyone from Harry S. Truman to Barbara Bush has gone looking for it. And y'know what they've found?

Nothing.

So let me tell you right now: I want to know where it is—and I want to know what's inside.

THE WORD *CORNERSTONE* itself has come to mean far more than just its purpose in a building.

By definition, a cornerstone is the very first piece of a building to be set into place. Its placement determines where everything else goes: The foundation is built outward from the cornerstone—the beginning place and the reference point. But when it comes to starting the construction of a building—and especially when constructing a *public* building—the laying of the cornerstone has also come to serve a symbolic and ceremonial purpose as well.

As the cornerstone is laid, dignitaries and officials gather. Speeches are made. Often a time capsule is buried near, or sometimes beneath, the cornerstone. Some cornerstones contain a hollow cavity that's lined with zinc to protect the time capsule. And generally, a plaque noting the date and time, and perhaps the names of those present, is affixed to the outer face of the stone for all to see.

Put all this together and you get a stone that announces: *This structure is being built for the ages.*

Now put yourself in 1792. The cornerstone is being laid for the White House — the residence of the president of the United States, on a site selected by George Washington himself.

How vital was the White House back then? Just as vital as it is today. In fact, to design it, a public competition was held. Among the entrants? Thomas Jefferson. (Jefferson submitted his entry under a false name.)

For our first few years, America had been governed from Philadelphia. But now this would be the first major government construction in the city that would serve as the nation's capital. The true seat of power for the United States.

WASHINGTON CORNERSTONES

AS WE SET OUT to find the cornerstone of the White House, we spoke to author and historian Jeanne Fogle, an expert on the structures that make Washington, DC, such a strikingly beautiful city. She quickly pointed out that the placement of a cornerstone can be structural, and also ceremonial.

Yet in the new city of Washington, DC, Fogle observed, cornerstones meant even more than that. These were not

ABOVE
THOMAS JEFFERSON
So important was the new presidential residence that a public competition was held to determine its design. Polymath and future president Thomas Jefferson submitted a design (under an assumed name) but didn't win the contest.

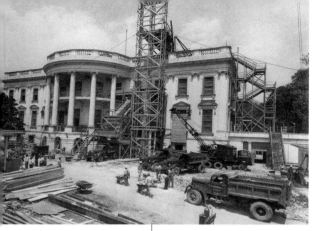

just new buildings being erected—this was a whole new *nation.* And more than that, the United States of America was a whole new *type* of nation. Nothing like America had ever been tried before in the history of the world. So, of course, the cornerstones of the buildings that would house the vibrant young nation's government would mean more than just symbolic blocks of stone.

In building the White House, they were building something exciting, something public, something dramatic. It's not hard to imagine the enthusiasm and anticipation as the competition was decided . . . as George Washington made some adjustments to the winning entry . . . and as the preliminary site preparations took place—all of it leading to the big moment: the laying of the foundational block—the cornerstone.

So what kind of ceremony do you think they would've had for *that*? Who do you think was on the guest list? Who do you think got to speak? Was there a time capsule—and if so, what was inside it? The answer to all of these questions, and to most others involving the White House cornerstone: *We just don't know.*

I'm not kidding. Other than a single newspaper account that was published a month after the stone was laid, there are no written records of the event.

But thanks to that newspaper story, we do know *when* the stone was laid: Saturday, October 13, 1792—though even that is sometimes disputed.

One legend says that the stone was laid on Columbus Day, October 12, and was put into place by George Washington himself. Good story, right? Unfortunately it's not true. George Washington was in Philadelphia at the time, and while 1792 was indeed the year that Columbus Day observances first began to be held (there was one in New York that year), the day had not achieved the holiday significance we currently know. So the first step in building the White House was *not* timed to coincide with Christopher Columbus's arrival in the Americas.

But it *may* have been timed to coincide with another anniversary.

IT'S ALWAYS THE FREEMASONS

WHEN IT COMES TO conspiracies surrounding American history, no group gets mentioned—and blamed—more than the Freemasons. It's no different here. Both James Hoban, the architect who won the design competition for the new executive mansion, and George Washington, who selected the site on which the mansion would be built, were Freemasons. Hoban himself, in fact, had founded the Washington Masonic Lodge that is still present today in Washington, DC.

Eight signers of the Declaration of Independence were Masons. Nine signers of the

"On Saturday the 13th inst. the first stone was laid in the south-west corner of the president's house, in the city of Washington, by the Free Masons of George-town and its vicinity, who assembled on the occasion. The procession was formed at the Fountain Inn, Georgetown. . . . The Ceremony was performed by brother Casaneva master of the lodge, who delivered an oration well adapted to the occasion."

— LETTER TO CHARLESTON *CITY GAZETTE*

U.S. Constitution. Five Chief Justices of the Supreme Court. And *15* times, they took the White House, from George Washington, to Teddy Roosevelt, FDR, Truman, LBJ, and Ford. So you tell me that this many people who helped shape our country's earliest days were also members of the same secret brotherhood, I want to know what that brotherhood stands for—and what it wants.

So what do Freemasons believe? There're only two requirements: 1) You have to believe in a Supreme Being. It can be any god, be it Christian, Jewish, Muslim, or any other. But you have to believe in God. And 2) you can't have a criminal record.

For centuries, the Freemasons have included the powerful among their membership—a membership devoted both to good works and adherence to traditional virtues, but also to the preservation of ancient knowledge and lore known only to their members. So what does this have to do with cornerstones? As the organization's name implies, trades that were associated with the art of *building*—much of it still resting upon techniques and principles that stretch back to the earliest days of civilization—played an important part in Freemasonry's founding and growth. The organization honors Euclid, the father of geometry, for the role geometry plays in accurate surveying, site lay-out, and building.

Among those construction principles, according to Scott Brown, an expert on the history of the White House and himself a Mason in the Washington, DC, lodge, is the location of a building's cornerstone. "We know the stone was laid Masonically," Brown told us, "and Masons always put the cornerstone in the northeast corner of a new building."

And yes, the Masonic organization is said to have amassed a large body of historical material, artifacts, items, and documents that they keep solely to themselves. To that end, Freemasonry has also been surrounded by rumors of hidden powers, and of perhaps even being the secret masters pulling the strings that guide the world.

Let me be clear: I don't believe that. But I do know it was the Freemasons who were there on that night in 1792 when the White House cornerstone was first set in place. So I was listening quite carefully when Brown suggested that the stone was actually removed from the building site and placed somewhere else for safekeeping. Where would they put it? And why take it?

Those are the questions that led us to one of the larg-est bodies of collected knowledge on Earth: the Library of Congress.

You'd think the Library of Congress, in Washington, DC, would have a substantial collection of documents related to the construction of the White House.

In reality, among all the hundreds of millions of books, magazines, newspapers, pamphlets, and virtually every other kind of information ever created, there is exactly *one* document dealing with the laying of the White House cornerstone. And that document is written *anonymously*.

The item in question is a copy of the Charleston *City Gazette*, dated October 20, 1792, just over a month after the cornerstone was laid. It is not an actual newspaper account that recorded the circumstances of the cornerstone being put into place. Rather, it was a letter attributed only to a "gentleman from Philadelphia." To see the full letter, see Exhibit 6A, and examine it for yourself.

BELOW
EXHIBIT 6A
A letter to the Charleston *City Gazette is the only existing published record of the laying of the White House cornerstone.*

SATURDAY, *October* 20, 1792.

CORNERSTONE.
SATURDAY, *October* 20, 1792.

Extract of a letter from a gentleman in Philadelphia, to his friend in Charleston, dated October 20, 1792.

"On Saturday the 13th inst, the first stone was laid in the south-west corner of the president's house, in the city of Washington, by the Free Masons of George-town and its vicinity, who assembled on the occasion. The procession was formed at the Fountain Inn, George-town, in the following order, viz.

1. The Free Masons, in masonic order.
2. The commissioners of the fed. building.
3. Gentlemen of the town & neighbourhood.
4. The different artificers, &c.

They proceeded in procession to the president's square. The ceremony was performed by brother Casaneva, master of the lodge, who delivered an oration well adapted to the occasion. Under the stone was laid a plate of polished brass, with the following inscription:

"This first Stone of the President's House was laid the 13th Day of October, 1792, and in the 17th Year of the Independence of the United States of America.

George Washington, *President.*
Thomas Johnston,
Doctor Stewart, } *Commissioners.*
Daniel Carroll,
James Hoban, *Architect.*
Collen Williamson, *Master-Mason.*
Vivat Respublica."

After the ceremony was performed they returned, in regular order, to Mr. Sutter's Fountain Inn, where an elegant dinner was provided, and the following toasts given in honor of the day:

1. The fifteen United States.
2. The President of the United States.
3. Our worthy brothers.
4. District of Columbia: may it flourish as the centre of the political and commercial interests of America.
5. The city of Washington: may time render it worthy of the name it bears.
6. Constitutional liberties of the people of the United States of America.
7. The French nation: a happy issue to their struggles for liberty and justice.
8. Marquis de la Fayette.
9. The masonic brethren throughout the universe.
10. The Rights of Man and the author of Common Sense.
11. The fair daughters of America.
12. The memory of those who have bled in the cause of liberty.
13. General Wayne and the western army: may their efforts be crowned by a speedy and honorable peace.
14. The governor and state of Maryland.
15. The governor and state of Virginia.
16. May peace, liberty and order extend from pole to pole.

The whole concluded with the greatest harmony and order."

And right there, in the very first line, is an answer to at least part of the mystery. Forget Masonic tradition and practice. The cornerstone was *never* placed in the northeast corner of the building, as is traditionally done. For some reason, it was put in the *southwest* corner. No explanation is given for the southwestern location of the stone, but there must have been one. Masons never do *anything* without a good, or at least arcane, reason.

But wait. It gets better.

According to the letter, the cornerstone did have a commemorative plate—one that was evidently not affixed to its exterior. The letter describes a brass plate that bore the following words:

> This first stone of the President's House was laid the 12th day of October 1792, and in the 17th Year of the Independence of the United States of America.
>
> **George Washington,**
> *President*
>
> **Thomas Johnson**
>
> **Doctor Stewart,**
> *Commissioners*
>
> **Daniel Carroll**
>
> **James Hoban,** *Architect*
>
> **Collen Williamson,**
> *Master Mason*
>
> **Vivat Respublica.**

With the exception of Thomas Johnson, all of the men listed were known to be Masons.

And did you note the discrepancy in the date? The letter makes clear that the stone was laid on Saturday, October 13, but the brass plate identifies *Friday, October 12,* as the date. Grand conspiracy? I don't think so. That one

strikes me as pretty easy to explain. The plate would have had to be fashioned and the inscription etched into its surface *before* the actual date for installing the stone. It seems likely that the 12th was the intended date for the ceremony. But there's another explanation that some find compelling.

ANOTHER EXPLANATION?

ON OCTOBER 13, 1307, Philip IV of France ordered the arrest of the leaders of the Knights Templar, a powerful medieval organization that many feel is closely related to the Freemasons, which developed far later.

With his order, Philip IV essentially destroyed the group . . . on Friday, the 13th. And yes, that led to the widespread, but probably inaccurate, belief that this event set in motion our superstitious Friday the 13th beliefs.

Few historians place credence in this theory of the origin of the Friday the 13th superstition. And not many more believe the almost equally widespread belief that the Knights Templar somehow went into hiding, preserving their special symbols and codes, and resurfaced as a new group, known as the Freemasons.

But keep that in mind the next time you hear about a Masonic conspiracy centered on Friday the 13th.

ABOVE
THE KNIGHTS TEMPLAR

On October 13, 1307, Philip IV of France ordered the arrest of the leaders of the Knights Templar, a powerful medieval organization that many feel is closely related to the Freemasons. Many were burned at the stake, but that failed to end the influence the group was thought to wield.

THIS PAGE RIGHT
THE CHOSEN ONES

The Knights Templar believed themselves to be special soldiers of the Lord, their religious fervor possibly enhanced by divinely inspired powers. They developed and used secret symbols and codes to communicate among themselves.

INSIDE THE TEMPLE

AS WE SEARCHED FOR the White House corner-stone, it was easy to find people who blamed it all on the Freemasons. We found folks who told us the Masons were part of the new world order—that their goal was to rule the world—and that they're even responsible for the deaths of others.

One of those people was filmmaker Chris Pinto, who has devoted a large portion of his life and career to investigating what he sees as the darker sides of secret societies, including the Freemasons.

As an example, Pinto cites the story of William Morgan, a Baptist minister who, in 1826, was kidnapped and murdered after announcing that he was going to expose the secrets of the Freemasons. Yet Pinto believes that while there are high-ranking Masons who extol many virtues, there is an inner circle of leaders who control and guide the organization toward far darker goals—goals that include world domination. That Mason who lives next door to you and whose lodge devotes itself to community good works is, according to Pinto, no more aware of the inner circle than is anybody else.

No question, that's an extreme view, written off by many, including myself. But let's not forget that the Freemasons *are* a secret society. They keep secrets. That's what they do. But do you want to know why the Masons really don't want to talk to most people (especially those with TV cameras)? Because everybody burns them. Everyone blames them for every bad thing that's happened in this world.

But as we began this search, we explained to the Freemasons what we were looking for. We showed them our evidence. We asked for their help. And guess what happened? They let us inside, making ours one of only three camera crews that were allowed to tape inside the Scottish Rite headquarters in Washington, DC, known as the House of the Temple. This was a once-in-a-lifetime chance to go right to the source.

Started in 1911, the HQ of Scottish Rite Freemasonry was modeled on the Persian tomb of Mausolus, the original mausoleum, which became one of the Seven Wonders of the Ancient World. It's got two giant limestone sphinxes that guard the entrance. The sphinxes have human faces but lions' bodies. And they represent two pillars of Masonic belief: wisdom and strength.

The building itself is a labyrinth of rooms and passageways. Symbols like the two-headed eagle, which represents power over east and west, decorate the walls. And you see symbols like pyramids and triangles everywhere. It's a nod to the Masons' origins as builders. The triangle, with its three sides, has been a sacred symbol for thousands of years. But to Masons, it reminds them of the three degrees of Masonry, the three orders of architecture. And for the Catholic Masons, it's a symbol of the Trinity: the Father, the Son, and the Holy Spirit.

The all-seeing eye is the Eye of Providence. It's the reminder to Masons that the Supreme Being watches and judges their words and actions. You'll see those on buildings, corporate logos, and even on the back of the dollar bill.

The biggest room is known as the Temple Room. It's where the Supreme Council convenes every two years to elect 33rd Degree Masons. Just outside is the seat where a guard is placed, in the Tyler's seat, to protect against non-Masons from entering. (See Exhibit 6B for photos of the Temple Room and Tyler's chair.) An inscription on the back of the chair says "Know thyself," which was written on ancient temples. Albert Pike, the father of modern-day Masonry, is always close by—because he's entombed in one of the building's walls.

As we toured through the House of the Temple, we found some of history's greatest artifacts: a flag that astronaut Neil Armstong took into space to the moon (Armstrong, John Glenn, and Buzz Aldrin were all Freemasons); the actual desk from J. Edgar Hoover's (also a Freemason) FBI office. And even a small stone from the White House.

For a moment, we thought this was it—especially when we saw the Masonic symbols—the compass and square—on the stone. How did this piece wind up in this headquarters of the Scottish Rite Freemasons?

It was sent there personally . . . by President Truman.

THE TRUMAN SHOW

ONE OF HIGHEST-RANKING MASONS to have been president of the United States was Harry S. Truman. The 33rd president became a Mason in 1909, and was a member of Grandview Lodge Number 618, of Grandview, Missouri. In the course of over a half century of Masonic membership, Truman is the only presidential Freemason to have celebrated a golden anniversary in the brotherhood; he reached the level of 33rd Degree Mason. That congruence—our 33rd president was a 33rd Degree Mason—has fed more than one conspiracy theory over the years.

Truman, incidentally, was proud and hardly secretive about his Freemason membership. He is reported to have claimed to be more proud of his rank within the Masons than he was of having been president. Not sure I believe that, but then again, Truman was well known for saying things provocatively in a way that no one ever expected.

So what's Truman's tie to the White House cornerstone? In 1949, during the Truman administration, the White House went through a substantial renovation, which is when they added what we know today as the Truman Balcony. The People's House had fallen into such disrepair that many people, if they knew its true condition, might have refused to live there. So as the building was being gutted all the way to its foundation, this struck many as the perfect time to make a concerted search for the cornerstone that had been missing since 1792.

During the search, they ran a World War II mine detector across the foundation of the White House. The device gave off its distinctive *ping-ping-ping,* indicating the presence of a metal object in the White House foundation.

This was it. The moment everyone was waiting for: Had they found

it? Had the cornerstone been located? We'll never know because Truman himself gave the word not to spend any more effort trying to locate the cornerstone. The location of the stone in question would make excavating it tricky, structurally questionable, and, perhaps most important of all, *expensive*. Truman was a notably frugal president, and he had enough problems with Congress without picking a fight over removing a stone that would either have to be put back in place or completely replaced afterward.

But there's another twist to the story. As the less structurally important walls of the White House were broken open during the renovation, Truman ordered that a block of stone from the executive mansion be sent to Masonic Temples all across the country—one block for one temple in each of the then 48 states. And here's the best part: Each of those stones from the White House—like the one in the Scottish Rite headquarters today—bore the construction mark of a working Freemason.

Easy to see how you could build a conspiracy out of something like that, right? But as we posed those questions to Freemason scholars and historians Arturo de Hoyos and S. Brent Morris, we didn't just find a surprising openness and candor—we found answers that actually made sense.

Why would anyone want to keep the location of such a stone a secret? they asked. "Why would you want to do that and not advertise it to the world that you found it? You would want to brag about it," Morris added. For most of us—as with the Freemasons—it'd be far more likely that you'd *celebrate* the rediscovery of such an important piece of our history, and do so with a bit of special pride that it was Freemasons who set the stone in the first place.

Starting to sound logical, right? But what if the cornerstone was filled with something powerful . . . or even mystical? And what about the code of secrecy that Freemasons agree to?

"You know, I wish I knew the powers that I had, being a member of this," Hoyos laughed, "because

when I received the thirty-third degree, I found out that I still had to pay for HBO and Cinemax." He went on to talk openly about the Morgan Affair that Freemason critics love to feature. He acknowledged that the murder might've happened because someone gave away Masonic secrets. It wasn't sanctioned by the Freemasons, though. It was "a group of people that did something stupid." So in Hoyos's eyes, when it came to the White House cornerstone, "If I'm going to admit to a Masonic murder per se, don't you think I'd tell you about some rock? I mean," he began to laugh, "we'd be happy to pull it out and parade it."

And what about all the secrecy?

"Sharing secrets, or sharing confidences, builds stronger relationships," Hoyos explained. So you can believe that Masons are trying to take over the world . . . or you can believe that this organization — whose libraries are open to any researcher who wants to come — is simply trying to build relationships and friendships they can count on.

But of all the things we heard in their headquarters, the biggest bombshell came when they asked why we weren't searching for the *other* missing cornerstone of democracy.

ANOTHER MISSING CORNERSTONE

"WHAT OTHER MISSING CORNERSTONE OF DEMOCRACY?" we asked.

The cornerstone of the Capitol building itself.

That's right. According to Hoyos and Morris, in addition to the White House, nobody knows the location of the Capitol's cornerstone, either.

For some expert insight, we turned to documentarian Jackson Polk, who has captured on film some of the efforts to locate the missing Capitol cornerstone—a cornerstone that *was* laid by George Washington himself.

In 1988, with the bicentennial of the Capitol approaching, the architect of the Capitol decided he wanted to locate the Capitol cornerstone. He quickly discovered that an independent effort to do so was already under way. Charlie Scalla, an air-conditioning mechanic for the Capitol, had become fascinated with the missing cornerstone and began searching, digging, and drilling in the cavernous basements of the Capitol, and doing so without any official permission.

UNDER THE CAPITOL

SCALLA'S ARCHAEOLOGICAL CURIOSITY WAS matched by his sense of how things work in Washington. When he was confronted by the Capitol architect about his freelance exploration of the Capitol's foundation, an

FACING PAGE TOP
A MASSIVE RENOVATION
The White House was gutted to its foundation during the Truman era renovation, but the cornerstone was never found.

FACING PAGE BOTTOM
STONES FOR MASONS
A worker make forms for concrete during the White House renovation. Truman ordered that blocks from stone walls broken during the renovation be sent to Masonic Temples all across the country. Each stone bore the construction mark of a working Freemason.

exploration the architect wanted stopped, Scalla was holding a very powerful set of cards. He had made several U.S. senators—who happened to be Freemasons—aware of his efforts, and the senators not only approved of his search, but instructed the architect to give Scalla every possible assistance he could.

According to Jackson Polk, Scalla was almost undoubtedly within six or eight feet of uncovering the Capitol cornerstone, deep beneath the Senate, when the word came down that the political reality had to be addressed. People in the House of Representatives were upset that the Senate was getting all the attention. There had been enough digging beneath the Senate. It was now the House's turn, and, for no other reason, the dig was moved.

Needless to say, the stone was never found.

Just silliness, right?

Still, as he showed us the actual footage, Polk believes that the Capitol cornerstone is exactly where George Washington placed it, not far from where Scalla was digging. Despite all the conspiracy theories, it hadn't been stolen or even hidden. It was just covered by the accumulation of additional construction, reinforcing stones, and other

materials over the course of two and a quarter centuries. And that's where it's likely to remain.

Which, according to Polk, isn't just a shame, but a tragedy. Today, we know that cornerstones were sometimes hollow, containing treasures—or even time capsules— from their time. Indeed, the cornerstone of the Washington Monument contains a Bible, along with dozens of documents and artifacts reflecting American life at the time. Now suppose the Capitol cornerstone contains a similar compartment. Imagine what sorts of things might've been placed there. Polk thinks there's a chance that such invaluable materials as alternate drafts of the Constitution itself could be resting within the stone. And yes, that's pure speculation—but until the stone is located and examined, we'll never know if the speculation has any basis in fact.

Incidentally, Polk believes that the location of the Capitol stone is in the *southeast* corner of the building. Not the northeast, where Freemasons traditionally place such stones. Why? It turns out that the tradition of placing the stone in the *northeast* corner didn't originate until after the year 1800—long after both of the stones from the Capitol and the White House had been placed.

That's one mystery decoded.

SO WHERE IS IT?

SO WHAT ABOUT THE White House cornerstone? Was it stolen? Was it dug up? Or did some inner circle of Freemasons somehow walk off with it in the night?

To find the answer, we relied on one of the most trustworthy of sources: math.

According to our best estimate, the White House cornerstone was about two feet high, six feet long, and two feet wide. Relying on her background as an engineer, Christine McKinley quickly took those 24 cubic feet, added the fact that granite is 150 pounds per cubic foot, and realized with or without whatever's inside it, we're talking about a stone that weighs 3,600 pounds. About the weight of a car. Even a *group* of thieves would have trouble moving that kind of hunk of stone secretly. They'd need a wagon, a team, pulleys, ropes—and above all—*time*.

So what happened to the cornerstone that everyone from Harry S. Truman to Barbara Bush went looking for? The most likely reality is that the stone wasn't stolen. The more we discovered about the missing White House cornerstone, the more sense it makes that the cornerstone is exactly where it always was—underneath the White House, where it wasn't just *placed* on that day in 1792. It was deliberately hidden.

To me, it's one of the few explanations that actually makes sense. Think about it. In 1792, America was still a brand-new country. We'd just defeated Great Britain, the world's greatest military power. Americans had to be counting the days until the British returned to take back what was once theirs. So maybe, at this exact moment, the bad guys were actually the good guys. Maybe the Freemasons—who were also patriots—put the cornerstone where nobody would

LAYING CORNER STONE WASHINGTON MONUMENT

ever find it—hiding it in such a way that it couldn't be identified by an invading and possibly marauding army.

The White House cornerstone was hidden in plain sight, and the decision to hide the commemorative plaque (which also still hasn't been found) may well have saved the stone from defacement—or actual theft—when the British did invade the United States again, during the War of 1812.

During that invasion, the White House was burned. You can still see scorch marks in certain places on its exterior. But the White House still stands, and it stands on a strong cornerstone located, I believe, in its *southeast* corner, exactly where it's always been, exactly where it's supposed to be.

When we first started this journey, the most important thing to me was to find that cornerstone, to put an end to the questions that some of the most powerful people in America have asked for more than 200 years. I now believe the cornerstone is still on the grounds of the White House, just where it was in 1792. And I don't believe the Masons ever stole it. But there's something far more important. If we had found the cornerstone and put it on display, it's just a rock under glass, like any other museum piece. It loses all of its symbolic power. But because the White House cornerstone is still—for all intents and purposes—missing, it retains its power as a symbol, and it keeps us wondering, thinking, and searching.

ABOVE

THE WASHINGTON MONUMENT

The cornerstone of the Washington Monument contains a Bible, along with dozens of documents and artifacts reflecting American life at the time. The question remains, when it comes to the White House cornerstone, was there anything hidden inside?

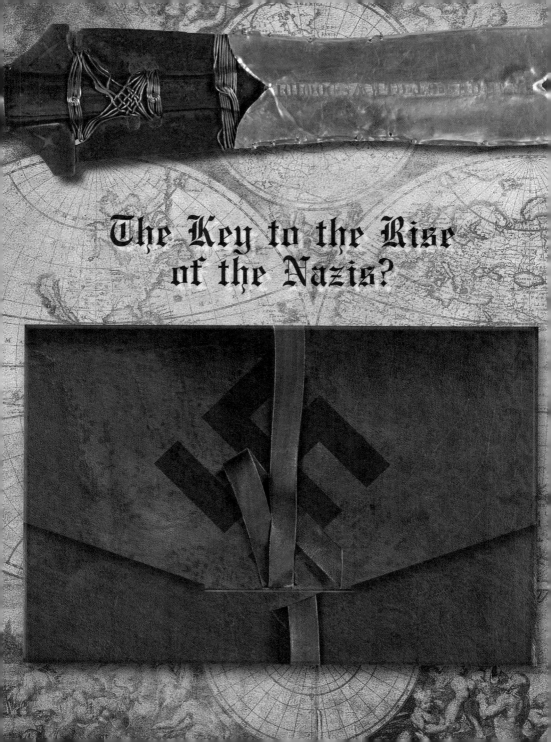

The Key to the Rise
of the Nazis?

THE SPEAR OF DESTINY: HISTORY'S MOST SACRED RELIC

WHAT IF I TOLD YOU that the Spear of Destiny—which was supposedly used to stab Christ on the cross—may also hold mystical powers—and that it's been pursued by everyone from Napoleon to Adolf Hitler?

Theories abound that the spear may allow its holder to become invincible. And some believe its final resting place may be in a sunken German U-boat off the coast of the United States. Let me be clear: I don't care if it has magic powers. You tell me that Adolf Hitler wanted this thing, I want to know what it is.

It's time to decode the Spear of Destiny.

The spear itself is mentioned only briefly in the Bible in John 19:34: "But one of the soldiers with a spear pierced his side, and forthwith came there out blood and water."

Just 19 words—and yet they form the heart of the story of the spear.

Over the centuries, that story gave birth to mystical lore that grew more and more elaborate. It began when Pontius Pilate sent Jesus to his death. It had to be confirmed that Christ had actually died, so a Roman soldier was ordered to stab him. This spear pierced his side, and it's said that blood and water seeped from his body. The soldier was unnamed in the Bible, though was later claimed to have been known as Longinus.

As a result of stabbing Christ, Longinus is said to have suffered for years. One story claims that he was subjected to a nightly mauling by a lion.

Because of the suffering Longinus experienced, and his repentance for the act of stabbing Jesus, some Christian faiths, including the Roman Catholic Church and Eastern Orthodox Church, refer to him as Saint Longinus. The weapon he wielded is itself occasionally referred to as the Spear of Longinus.

Other names for the spear include:

- the Holy Lance

- the Lance of Longinus

- the Spear of Christ

By any of its names, though, the true spear would be among the most revered and coveted of all religious artifacts. Indeed, for centuries, many have believed that Longinus's spear controls the destiny of this world, for good or for evil. For that reason, conquerors and would-be world leaders were among those who coveted it most highly.

So where did the spear go?

It depends on which spear you're talking about. Throughout history, there have been several relics said to be the Spear of Destiny. In fact, today there are no fewer than *three* Spears of Destiny that we know of, two of them in prominent locations: one in the Vatican and one in Vienna, Austria.

For obvious reasons, we started by searching for the spear in the Vatican.

Unfortunately, the Vatican spear isn't on display. According to historian Elizabeth Lev, it's only taken out once a year for a few moments at the end of the day on Good Friday. No exceptions.

In fact, the Vatican spear is so treasured, it's located in one of the most prominent pieces of real estate in all of religion: Saint Peter's Basilica, the burial place of the apostle Peter, who became the very first pope. The spear—along with a series of other relics—makes the framework for the tomb of Saint Peter.

As Lev explained, the spear is ceremonially removed once a year from its place of honor, and almost immediately replaced. But no matter how

UNDER THE VATICAN

Saint Peter, one of Jesus's 12 apostles, helped lead Christ's followers after the Crucifixion.

Saint Peter traveled to Rome, and in 64 CE, he was martyred by crucifixion and then buried. Three hundred years later, Saint Peter's Basilica, the centerpiece of the Vatican, was built over the grave site of the man who became the first pope.

At the heart of the basilica, 60 feet below the altar, is the body of Saint Peter. And then, located around it on the piers that are holding up the dome, are four chapels that have contained four of the most important relics of Christianity:

- The veil that wiped Christ's face when he was on the Cross

- A piece of the true Cross

- The head of Saint Peter's brother, Saint Andrew (returned to Greece in 1964 by Pope Paul VI)

- The Spear of Destiny (the one presented to Pope Innocent VIII as a bribe)

See Exhibit 5A (page 107) for a map of the Vatican Grottos.

LEFT
THE TOMB OF SAINT PETER
The chapels surrounding Peter's tomb contained four of Christianity's most sacred relics.

many times we asked, there was no way the Vatican was going to let us test the authenticity of its spear.

Nevertheless, Lev believes that the Vatican spear is of "a good pedigree," and could very well be the real thing.

Theologian Jason Spiehler adamantly disagrees. According to him, toward the end of the 1400s, the Vatican spear "was given by a sultan to Pope Innocent VIII. Why? Because he wants the pope to keep his brother as a political prisoner."

For sure, it's one of the wilder stories. The pope had a sultan locked in jail, hoping that the sultan's little brother would give the pope the most valuable thing he had: a relic that he claimed was the real Spear of Destiny. It was a total bribe, but here's the kicker: The younger brother wasn't bribing the pope to get his big brother *out* of jail, he was bribing the pope to keep his big brother *in* jail, so that the younger brother could be the sultan.

According to Spiehler, there's no way the young sultan would have traded away what was potentially the most powerful religious relic in Christendom just to keep his brother in jail. I mean, if he had possession of the true spear, why would he even fear his older brother? Think about it: If *you* had the true spear, would you trade it away?

Exactly. Which means it's far more likely that what the sultan really gave the pope was potentially a convincing *replica* of the spear.

Still, regardless of whether it was the real spear or not—and regardless of whether it had magic powers— one thing became very clear: The spear clearly had a political function. And Pope Innocent VIII wasn't the only one to realize this.

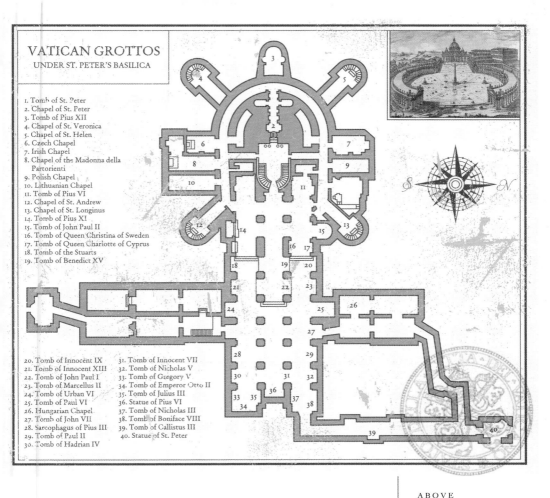

VATICAN GROTTOS
UNDER ST. PETER'S BASILICA

1. Tomb of St. Peter
2. Chapel of St. Peter
3. Tomb of Pius XII
4. Chapel of St. Veronica
5. Chapel of St. Helen
6. Czech Chapel
7. Irish Chapel
8. Chapel of the Madonna della Partorienti
9. Polish Chapel
10. Lithuanian Chapel
11. Tomb of Pius VI
12. Chapel of St. Andrew
13. Chapel of St. Longinus
14. Tomb of Pius XI
15. Tomb of John Paul II
16. Tomb of Queen Christina of Sweden
17. Tomb of Queen Charlotte of Cyprus
18. Tomb of the Stuarts
19. Tomb of Benedict XV

20. Tomb of Innocent IX
21. Tomb of Innocent XIII
22. Tomb of John Paul I
23. Tomb of Marcellus II
24. Tomb of Urban VI
25. Tomb of Paul VI
26. Hungarian Chapel
27. Tomb of John VII
28. Sarcophagus of Pius III
29. Tomb of Paul II
30. Tomb of Hadrian IV

31. Tomb of Innocent VII
32. Tomb of Nicholas V
33. Tomb of Gregory V
34. Tomb of Emperor Otto II
35. Tomb of Julius III
36. Statue of Pius VI
37. Tomb of Nicholas III
38. Tomb of Boniface VIII
39. Tomb of Callistus III
40. Statue of St. Peter

OVER THE CENTURIES, the Spear of Destiny is said to have passed through the hands of at least 45 leaders:

- Constantine the Great possessed the spear and supposedly became the foremost general of his time, founding the Eastern Roman Empire.

- Charlemagne supposedly used the spear to conquer Italy and unite most of Western Europe.

ABOVE
EXHIBIT 5A
Map of Vatican grottos

- Otto I successfully defended Hungarian raids into Saxony.

Sounds crazy, right? But think about this: Otto I, founder of the Holy Roman Empire, was said to have never been defeated in battle. And yes, maybe his unbroken string of victories was the result of his military skills and the size of his armies—but that didn't stop others from thinking that the Spear of Destiny was the source of his triumphs. More important, if a power-crazed megalomaniac thinks that an ancient religious relic can grant him absolute power, you can bet that he's going to do everything he can to get his hands on it.

No matter the cost.

The same goes for *protecting* the spear. In fact, when Napoleon's armies were approaching Vienna early in the 1800s, the city fathers ordered the spear moved to Nuremberg. They were willing to move one of the city's most prized possessions, its holiest treasure, to another city in order to keep it from falling into the hands of a man who already seemed poised to conquer the world. Holding the spear might make Napoleon completely unstoppable.

Which brings us back to Hitler—who was clearly looking to steal a page from the super-villain playbook.

HITLER AND THE SPEAR

ADOLF HITLER WAS SAID TO HAVE first seen the spear in Vienna, in a museum. But know this: There are almost as many legends about Hitler's relationship to the Spear of Destiny—and its promise of near-infinite power—as there are surrounding the spear itself.

Many of those legends come solely from a 1973 book by Trevor Ravenscroft, *The Spear of Destiny*, which claims that Hitler first saw the spear in Vienna, where it had been returned after the Napoleonic Wars. Hitler was a boy at the time, but was already dreaming of world conquest. What sort of kid dreams of conquering the world? The kind who grows up to be Adolf Hitler.

The way Ravenscroft tells the story, upon seeing the spear, the young Hitler was seized by a mystical vision that foretold his possession of the spear and its use to help him conquer the world.

But Ravenscroft goes even further, arguing that Adolf Hitler's ruthless rise to power, and his actual launching of World War II, were all undertaken to capture the spear. According to him, everything else was secondary to getting the Spear of Destiny into Hitler's possession.

OK. Time out. Let's just be clear here. No question, that's taking the crazy a bit too far. Even a quick look will tell you that there are no credible historians who take Ravenscroft and his theories seriously.

Of course, there are *plenty* of Ravenscroft enthusiasts all over the Internet, but secondhand Ravenscroft is even wackier than the original. However, we do owe Ravenscroft's book for one thing: The screenwriter of *Raiders of the Lost Ark* used it as part of the movie's plot.

BELOW

ADOLF HITLER

Adolf Hitler had a lifelong obsession with the Spear of Destiny. He was said to have first seen it as a boy, in a museum in Vienna.

THE THULE SOCIETY

The Thule Society was built upon beliefs that stretched back to the early German myths: of men with the powers of gods . . . men who were better than all other men . . . a super-race. Those who joined the Thule Society had to sign a blood oath, asserting the truth of horrifying lines like this: "The signer hereby swears to the best of his knowledge and belief that no Jewish or colored blood flows in either his or in his wife's veins, and that among their ancestors are no members of the colored races." (See Exhibit 5B, below.)

The emblem of the Thule Society inspired the Nazis to use a swastika as their symbol, and Hitler dedicated *Mein Kampf* to a Thule member. It was this occult group that selected a young man named Adolf Hitler to be their leader, and it is said that with the Spear of Destiny in their possession, they believed they would become invincible.

Even the twin lightning bolt insignia of the SS, based on an ancient German rune, has been compared to spears.

RIGHT

EXHIBIT 5B

The signer hereby swears to the best of his knowledge and belief that no Jewish or colored blood flows in either his or in his wife's veins, and that among their ancestors are no members of the colored races.

Still, one giant question remains: What happened to the actual spear?

In October 1938, the lance that Hitler believed to be the Spear of Destiny was in a Viennese museum. With Austria now under Nazi control, Hitler supposedly ordered the SS to seize the relic and move it by train to Nuremberg. He stored it in a church for six years, the amount of time it took his engineers to secretly build a specially constructed vault—a vault capable of standing up to Allied bombing, protecting the spear and the power Hitler may have believed it possessed.

For me, here's the heart of the story: Real or fake—whether it had mystical powers or not—if this object is being chased by the most evil man of all time, I want to know more about it. Yet the more we searched, the more we realized that there was one person who might've been even more obsessed with the spear than Hitler himself: Heinrich Himmler.

Trained as an agronomist, Himmler was also deeply committed to both the study of the occult and the attempt to put occult forces to work for the darkest goals of the Third Reich. Those forces included the power of the Spear of Destiny.

Heinrich Himmler was the head of the SS, Hitler's most elite military group. He was also the man behind the horrors of the extermination camps, where more than eleven million Jews and other minority groups were gassed, cremated, and worked to death in the single most horrible and most chillingly efficient mass murder campaign the world has ever seen.

But the spear was far from the only focus of Heinrich Himmler's obsession. A self-styled "intellectual," Himmler developed and promoted any number of "theories" explaining the superiority of the Aryan people. The Aryans, Himmler believed, were meant to rule the world—and impose their superiority upon it.

And ready for creepy nuttiness? He believed that Germans were superior to all other people, and put that belief to the test by tracking down the burial places of great heroes from the Aryan past. Such graveyards were designated "breeding cemeteries" because they thought babies who were conceived in graveyards would inherit the attributes of the heroes buried there. That's right. They were trying to make babies in cemeteries.

Most important, Himmler was an ardent member of the Thule Society, a group dedicated to both mysticism and the superiority of the Aryan race.

ABOVE
HEINRICH HIMMLER
Here's the one person who might've been even more obsessed with the spear than Hitler himself: Heinrich Himmler.

Himmler took his fascination with the occult so far, he had a precise replica of the spear made for his private office, where he kept it near a vial of his own blood. And yes, a vial of your own blood is easily the worst paperweight ever.

So what happened to Himmler? He killed himself in prison after the war, rather than standing up to face his accusers and accepting punishment for his crimes. So much for the super-German.

Yet before he was captured, before the Third Reich fell to the Allies, Himmler may have put into place a mystical plan involving the Spear of Destiny, German submarines . . . and Antarctica. Which again takes us back to the only question that matters: Where is Hitler's spear today?

ANTARCTICA

ACCORDING TO HISTORIAN and Nazi researcher Dieter Maier, at the end of World War II, the Germans were mounting submarine expeditions to Antarctica, shipping "important objects and important people" there "to preserve the Fourth German Reich to strike back at any given moment."

Is that even true? It is.

Without question, at the end of World War II, the Nazis started to lay the groundwork for their own comeback. There's concrete evidence that Hitler sent U-boats to various locations around the globe — including Antarctica — to set up bases across the ice. Rumors of these secret bases on the frozen continent, perhaps used as storehouses for secret research materials, stolen artworks, wealth, and treasure, began circulating even before the end of the war. Hitler was trying to give the Fourth Reich the ability to succeed where the Third Reich had failed.

But with the war drawing toward its inevitable close in 1945, other rumors began to circulate. German U-boats had been sneaking secretly to the coast of the United States, putting spies and saboteurs ashore in Maine, Long Island, and North Carolina, clearly working their way down the East Coast. What were they after? Among other things, the secrets of the Manhattan Project. Oh yes. The Nazis were going after the plans for the atomic bomb. The spies dropped on Long Island managed to remain hidden in New York for almost a month before they were captured.

Yet according to Maier, there may have been another agenda at work aboard the U-boats. He believes it's possible that with the Reich collapsing around them, Germans, including Heinrich Himmler, may have hatched a scheme to leave behind a fake Spear of Destiny, while smuggling what they believed to be the true spear out of Germany. Their goal? To hide it in a secret Antarctic location, where it, and its powers, could be used to launch a rebirth of the Nazis—a Fourth Reich—when the time was right. The journey down the East Coast was only part of the voyage—the U-boats' actual goal was farther south. *Much* farther south. As in Antarctica.

Yet what's most disturbing about Maier's assertion isn't just the ongoing existence of neo-Nazis

BELOW
THE FROZEN
CONTINENT
Some believe the Nazis planned to smuggle the Spear of Destiny out of Germany, hoping to hide it in a secret Antarctic location, where, when the time was right, it could be used to launch a Fourth Reich.

While the legend says that he who holds the Spear of Destiny is invincible, here's the flip side: He who loses the spear loses his life.

and modern-day followers of Hitler—it's their belief that the spear's real power could be used today. This belief was further clarified by biblical scholar Dr. Erhard Zauner, who said that "they wanted to present Hitler as the leader of the world. The new God."

Please tell me you're paying attention here. According to Dr. Zauner, Nazi occultists supposedly believed getting the spear in the hands of Hitler wouldn't just symbolize his leadership and make him an unstoppable force in war. With the Spear of Destiny, Hitler would become more than the Führer—he'd become God himself.

Let me be crystal clear here: I'm not worried about the spear having magical powers. But what I am worried about is a small group of modern neo-Nazis who believe in those powers. And will fight for those powers. You see, it doesn't matter if they're wrong. From 9/11 to recent shootings here in the United States, there's nothing more dangerous than a true believer on his own crazy mission.

SO. BACK TO THE LOCATION OF THE SPEAR. If there is any accuracy to Maier's speculation, it would mean that the spear captured by the Allies was most likely the replica that Himmler had stored in his office. Or even another replica. Historian Peter Levenda pointed out that the Nazis created a virtual industry out of counterfeiting works of art and rare artifacts, including religious relics. After the war,

FACING PAGE
NAZI SPOILS
Knowing that the Allies would recapture plundered art treasures, Himmler may have planted a fake spear in order to keep the location of the real one secretly in Nazi hands.

many of the artworks that were returned to their owners turned out to be counterfeits—and it could very well be that the spear captured by the Allies, which now sits in the museum known as the Vienna Hofburg, is among the fakes.

The only way to find out for sure is to test the spear in Vienna. But when we tried, that also proved to be impossible.

However, we were able to arrange for an exact replica of the Vienna spear to be examined by an archaeo-metallurgist, a scientific expert on ancient metals. But after X-raying its metal pieces, Mathias Mehofer was only able to determine that the material is "very old." To get more precise and accurate figures for the age of the spear would require carbon dating, which would require removing as much as a half centimeter of material from the spear. Much as we'd love to do it, the museum wouldn't allow it.

So with no means of scientifically dating the age of the spear that's in the Vienna Hofburg, there's obviously no way of knowing if it even *could* be the true Spear of Destiny.

In my mind, though, I don't think it's the real spear. To me, it's a replica—and whether it's the one Himmler commissioned or yet another, we have no way of knowing.

Yet that doesn't mean that there aren't some very strange stories surrounding it, some of them dating to its recapture by the Allies.

While the legend says that he who holds the Spear of Destiny is invincible, here's the flip side: He who loses the spear loses his life.

Those believers look to Hitler to prove their point. Because two hours

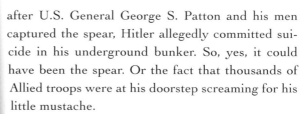

HITLER DEAD

Fuehrer Fell at CP, German Radio Says;
Doenitz at Helm, Vows War Will Continue

Churchill
Hints Peace
Is at Hand

BELOW
GEORGE S.
PATTON

*The Spear of Destiny
was found in Nuremburg
by invading U.S. troops,
and returned to Austria
by American General
George S. Patton after
World War II. Patton
died soon after.*

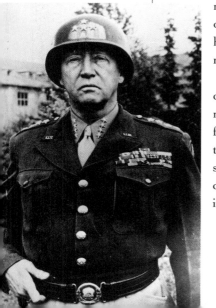

after U.S. General George S. Patton and his men captured the spear, Hitler allegedly committed suicide in his underground bunker. So, yes, it could have been the spear. Or the fact that thousands of Allied troops were at his doorstep screaming for his little mustache.

To this day, we don't know whether or not the American troops who took possession of the spear believed in the legends surrounding it—or were even *aware* of those legends. But we do know that the Allied commander who was ultimately in charge of the occupation forces in that part of Germany certainly knew of the spear and had in fact given it some thought of his own.

GEORGE S. PATTON

IN ADDITION to being a brilliant and controversial battlefield commander, Patton was a strong believer in reincarnation. In his poem "Through a Glass, Darkly," he recounted his numerous former lives. And ironically, one of those lives may have been lived as Longinus himself. *"Perhaps I stabbed our Savior,"* he wrote, clearly referring to Longinus's infamous deed.

Pretty spooky, right? Here's an even spookier one: As part of the occupation, Patton oversaw the return of stolen artworks and relics to their rightful owners. In the case of the Spear of Destiny, the rightful owner was Austria, from whom the spear was taken by Hitler years before. Patton had ordered that the spear be returned to Vienna, where it resides in a museum to this day.

And here's the twist. Not long after the spear was released from Patton's control, the great general was killed as a result of a freak, slow-speed car accident.

One more chapter in the strange history of the spear.

SO IF WE RULE OUT THE VATICAN SPEAR and the one in Vienna, that leaves one final theory to investigate: What about that supposed Antarctic base? It's more real than you realize, though its purpose remains unknown. A *New York Times* article from July 1945 mentions the discovery of a secret Nazi "Antarctic haven." Another source said 16 crew members landed on the Antarctic shore and deposited numerous boxes that apparently held documents and relics from the Third Reich. A U.S. military operation called Operation High Jump soon followed. The operation had numerous objectives, ranging from testing equipment in frigid conditions to the

establishment of a research facility. It was also alleged that Operation High Jump had another purpose: to seek out and demolish a Nazi base.

Which raises the question: Back in 1945, if you were looking for a place to hide the most precious and potentially powerful relic in your possession, where would *you* hide it? No question, Antarctica wouldn't be a bad choice, especially back then, when it was largely unexplored, hard to get to, and difficult to survive in. Y'know what I call a place like that? The last place anybody would look.

And that may just be exactly what the Nazis were hoping for: a place almost impossibly remote and inhospitable, where they could hide the Spear of Destiny and its powers while they put into motion their darkest and most dangerous plan yet.

But here's the twist. That U-boat that was supposedly bound for Antarctica? It never reached its destination. It was sunk off the coast of Florida, where its hulk still rests today—and where, perhaps, the true Spear of Destiny rests with it.

MY OWN SPEAR STORY

YOU THINK WE'RE DONE NOW, RIGHT?

We're not.

Because I'm going to do something we don't do in any other part of this book. I want to tell you my personal tie to the Spear of Destiny.

Years ago, I was contacted by Chris Blake, a man who said he had some delicate information to share with me. He

According to the story, the Sons of the Fallen believe that when the Temple is rebuilt in Jerusalem, they will send their hand-picked man into the Temple — the Holy of Holies — with the Spear of Destiny.

told me about a plot that would have severe repercussions if it was carried out. Of course, we verified key elements of Blake's story with the police to make sure it checked out.

Blake was a personal driver and bodyguard for a wealthy and powerful man. How powerful? His boss was a friend — and had the ear — of a U.S. president.

According to Blake, his wealthy boss — whom he's keeping anonymous out of respect for him — apparently knew the location of the true Spear of Destiny.

In the course of his service to his boss, Blake encountered many other people, including a high-ranking government official who, one night, struck up a conversation over drinks. As Blake tells the story, the federal official worked the conversation around to the Spear of Destiny, and then asked the biggest and most frightening bar-story question Blake had ever heard: "What would you say if I told you that your boss is the man who stole the Spear of Destiny from Adolf Hitler?"

To say that Blake was stunned is of course an understatement. But as the government official continued to speak, the story took on more frightening details.

According to the official, Blake's boss was a member of a secret group calling themselves the *B'nai ha Nephilim*—the "Sons of the Fallen."

Disciples of Lucifer.

"And just so that you understand," Blake explained, "they believe that the God of the Bible is evil. And they believe that Lucifer is good."

I know. I had the same reaction. But stay with me a moment. This small, powerful group believes that the God that we all know is the bad guy in the story.

According to the story, the Sons of the Fallen believe that when the Temple is rebuilt in Jerusalem, they will send their handpicked man into the Temple—the Holy of Holies—with the Spear of Destiny. There, he will shed his own blood with the spear and then proclaim himself the Messiah. The Sons of the Fallen "plan on ruling the world. They believe it enough to not only be willing to kill for it. They believe it enough to die for it."

Even now, according to Blake, the Sons of the Fallen are at work in Jerusalem, attempting to bring the Temple into being—so they can put their plan into motion.

Insanity, right?

But here's the detail I care about: Blake doesn't believe the story. He doesn't think Lucifer is the *good guy*. He agrees that whether it's true or not . . . that part doesn't matter. What matters is the idea that these people *still exist today*.

And that may be the most terrifying plan of all for the spear.

BELOW

FALLEN ANGELS

Is there a secret group out there that follows Lucifer and believes that with the power of the Spear of Destiny its own messiah will rule the world? Some say such a group exists, and is called the B'nai ha Nephilim —*the "Sons of the Fallen."*

CONCLUSION

TO ME, WHETHER THE SPEAR OF DESTINY gives an army unstoppable power is almost irrelevant. If it makes an army *believe* it's unstoppable, then that's power enough. I used to see the cost of that power every Thanksgiving when my wife's Uncle Charles visited us.

Charles was a teenager when the Nazis brought him to a concentration camp. He weighed 158 pounds; by the end of the war, he was 66 pounds. He saw the gas chambers himself, and the crematorium, and he knew what it was for. It was an oven to melt people. So, nothing terrifies me like the idea that a Fourth Reich might be back to finish the job. Indeed, history has shown us that whenever groups try to gain that level of power, it's rarely put to good use.

While going on this quest, we discovered that no one really knows where the true Spear of Destiny is. But we also found out this—the one fact no one knew: There are still people looking for it.

So next time you watch a story about fanatics and their quest for power, I promise, you won't look at that story the same way again.

DISEGNI·DI·MACHINE·ET·

DELLE·ARTI·SECRETI·

ET·ALTRE·COSE·

DI·LEONARDO·DA·VINCI

RACOLTI   DA

POMPEO LEO
NI

Leonardo da
Vinci

THE REAL DA VINCI CODE: DID LEONARDO PREDICT AN APOCALYPSE?

WHAT IF I TOLD YOU that the secrets of our future—our fate—may be found in the work of Leonardo da Vinci?

Leonardo da Vinci is considered by many scholars to be the greatest painter of all time, producing both the *Mona Lisa* and *The Last Supper.*

Da Vinci was the ultimate Renaissance man. Artist, botanist, architect, scientist, mathematician, writer, musician . . . you name it, Da Vinci did it. And he did it at a level that boggles the mind. As an inventor, Da Vinci accurately predicted hundreds of advancements in science, transportation, medicine, and warfare . . . 500 years *before they happened.*

Some call that human genius—but a few think he actually *saw* the future . . . and many now believe that Da Vinci's most dangerous prophecy has yet to be unlocked. A Da Vinci drawing that was hidden for centuries may prove to be the final piece to Da Vinci's most important prophecy.

It's time to head to Italy. We're trying to decode Leonardo da Vinci.

Born out of wedlock in 1452 to a wealthy notary father and a peasant mother, Da Vinci was just 14 years old when he had his first painting apprenticeship with Renaissance master Andrea del Verrocchio. According to the story, one of his first big opportunities was to paint an angel in the great master's work *The Baptism of Christ*. After looking at it, Verrocchio allegedly vowed that he would never paint again, unable to live up to his young student Leonardo da Vinci.

No question, Leonardo da Vinci was the very definition of a "Renaissance man." But a literal *prophet*? A man who foresaw our own world and the potential disasters facing it in precise and specific detail—and foresaw them 500 years ago? How's that even possible?

Yet that possibility is *exactly* what a small group of people claim—and their claims are based on a single page from one of the most mysterious of all of Da Vinci's works: the *Codex Atlanticus*.

Hidden for centuries, that page may be the most important clue to Da Vinci's secret beliefs—and perhaps to his prophecies.

THE CODEX ATLANTICUS

TO EXPLAIN THE *CODEX ATLANTICUS*, first you need to know what a codex is. Simply put, it's a collection of ancient works. In that context, the *Codex Atlanticus* is essentially Da Vinci's brain on paper. You see, throughout his life, whatever specific project he

> *At some point in history, something on page 1033 was removed. Many thought it was lost to history. No one knew who took it; no one knew what had happened to it; no one knew exactly what was missing.*

was working on, Da Vinci was constantly making notes, filling thousands of loose pages, as well as the pages of notebooks, with every idea he came up with . . . every observation he made. These working notebooks and papers were the catchalls for his ideas and visions.

Had the pages of his notes and sketches been left in his studio, they might've been scattered, lost to history.

But those pages weren't left loose. Rather, after his death, his personal journals, sketches, philosophies, and inventions were gathered by admirers and bound into volumes. Such a volume is called a codex, and Da Vinci's codices are among the most valuable in all of history.

How valuable? One of the lesser codices, known as the *Codex Leicester*, focusing primarily on Da Vinci's later scientific writings and notations, and containing only 72 pages, was purchased in 1994 for $30 million. The buyer? Another visionary: Microsoft founder Bill Gates.

Far greater than the *Codex Leicester*, though, was the set of volumes known as the *Codex Atlanticus*, more than 1,000 pages of Da Vinci brilliance and insight, bound into 12 volumes. Conservative estimates place a value upon these volumes at more than $700 million.

BELOW
THE CODEX LEICESTER
Da Vinci's 72-page Codex Leicester, *focusing primarily on his later scientific writings and notations, was purchased for $30 million in 1994 by Bill Gates.*

Of those pages, one stands out as strikingly provocative, even among Da Vinci's works: page 1033 of the *Codex Atlanticus*. To many, it is the most wildly apocalyptic work Da Vinci ever created . . . a stark vision of the end of the world and the death of humanity. But to a few, page 1033 doesn't just describe an apocalypse. It predicts one.

In the *Codex Atlanticus*, one of the things most interesting about page 1033 is what's *missing*. Not missing from the page's content, but from a pride-of-place position affixed to it.

At some point in history, something on page 1033 was removed. Many thought it was lost to history. No one knew who took it; no one knew what had happened to it; no one knew exactly what was missing.

But an unexpected discovery showed the path that the missing piece had followed for at least the past century and a half.

The part turned out to be nothing less than the earliest known self-portrait of Da Vinci himself. It had come into the possession of Cardinal Placido Maria Tadini, Archbishop of Genoa, a man who numbered among his responsibilities the suppression of potential rebellions against religion.

For reasons unknown, Cardinal Tadini hid the drawing, placing it within the cover of an otherwise undistinguished book. He died in 1847, and his home and possessions were sold at auction. The new owners settled into the cardinal's home, and if they ever examined the ancient book, they clearly didn't examine it closely.

It wasn't until 1940, when a descendant of the owners moved into new quarters, and the house's contents were also moved, that someone finally noticed something unusual about the book. Looking closely at the volume, he discovered the drawing hidden within it. But did he realize it was drawn by Da Vinci? Of course not. Still, he had taste. Finding the drawing attractive, the new owner framed it and hung it on a wall.

There it remained for decades . . . until it was noticed by art collector Cristina Gerbino's family friend, an antiques restorer who felt that he had spotted something exceptional—and perhaps even more than that.

After some scientific and historical testing, Gerbino realized that this was, indeed, the work of Leonardo da Vinci. The drawing's dimensions perfectly matched those of the missing part of the *Codex Atlanticus*. The paper and the ink were of the sort that Da Vinci used. Even the glue could be matched to the spine of the book. And the signature at the bottom? We were lucky enough to have Gerbino show us the page personally: "This is a picture of the lower part of our drawing. So if we read the signature from the left side to the right side, we have two letters that are very clear, *E-O*. *Eo* is 'myself' in Italian. Then we have four letters together. *N-A-R-D*. NARD. Then we have *O-D-A*. Leonardo da Vinci. Myself, Leonardo da Vinci. It's a signature. Then we can read the signature from the right side to the left side. And our interpretation is if we translate that in English it reads, 'In this way, I do this myself.' "

MIRROR WRITING

THE FACT THAT THE SIGNATURE READS BACKWARD is a telltale sign that we're likely looking at a real Da Vinci. He wrote almost all his personal letters in mirror writing (the sentences must be read right-to-left

FACING PAGE
**BODY
FASCINATION**
Da Vinci's fascination with human anatomy inspired him to focus his talents on sometimes macabre subjects, as in this study of a hanged man.

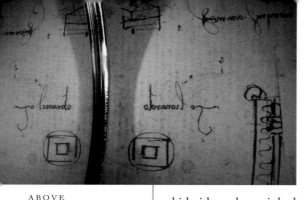

ABOVE
MIRROR WRITING
*Da Vinci wrote almost
all his personal letters
in mirror writing
(right-to-left rather
than left-to-right). For
reasons unknown, the
signature on the drawing
was erased—perhaps
the owner feared that if
Da Vinci's distinctive
signature was visible, the
treasured drawing would
be taken away from
him. But enough of an
impression of Da Vinci's
mirror writing remained
to be traced, the same
way private eyes in the
movies can trace the
impression of writing
on a notepad's blank
page after the top page
has been torn off. Pretty
sneaky—but also pretty
easy to trace. Here, the
mirror-written signature
of Leonardo da Vinci can
be read as "In this way,
I do this myself."*

rather than left-to-right). Some say it was because he was a southpaw and he simply didn't want to smudge the ink. Others say it was so lesser artists wouldn't copy his masterworks.

But many believe it was to hide ideas that might have gotten him in trouble with the government, the law, or the Church. You see, in Da Vinci's time, dissecting anything more than a pig was strictly forbidden. But Da Vinci performed clandestine dissections of humans and created highly detailed anatomical diagrams and writings, all in mirror writing.

As a matter of fact, even the mirror version of his own signature contains a coded message. Read one way, the signature is his name: *Leonardo.*

But by focusing on the individual letters and combinations of letters that make up his name, we can also translate the reversed signature as: *In this way, I do this myself.*

It doesn't sound too provocative, but keep in mind this was the 1400s. This was a time when self-reliance and putting *human reason* first were considered a threat to the Church. The Church always was supposed to come first, and humans were just its obedient servants. So between chopping up human corpses and the idea that the human body might be a marvel of science (and not God), those were two things that may have put Da Vinci on a short list of people to keep a close, watchful, and potentially suppressive eye on.

Oh, and to see how hard mirror writing is, try it yourself. Try writing your first name backward forming the letters as they are normally formed. Not too difficult, right?

Now try writing your name backward while reversing the direction in which the letters face. (To see what the results should look like, write your name the normal way and then hold the page in front of a mirror. The reflection will show you what you're going to try to re-create.)

If your name happens to be Otto, you've got it made. But the rest of us aren't going to have it as easy.

So why is page 1033 of the *Codex Atlanticus* so special? According to Gerbino, "That page tells about prophecies." It's the only page in the entire codex that mentions a prophecy. And yes, something on that one page — page 1033 — was purposely removed and hidden by the cardinal.

And now you see why this drawing matters. Many people believe page 1033 is Da Vinci trying to tell the world something about its future. Make no mistake: His predictions are grim.

Da Vinci writes of entire forests being destroyed and of weapons of mass destruction. He refers to the extinction of species and the slaughter of man. One of his most recurring themes is destruction by water, flood, or tidal wave.

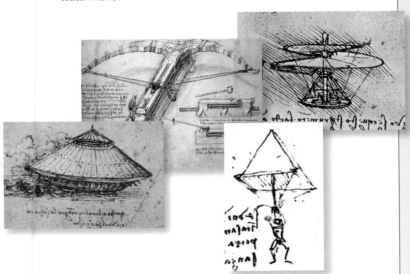

Another Renaissance artist who was thought to use secret language was Michelangelo. It is reported that the Sistine Chapel contains coded messages consisting of Hebrew letters and Old Testament symbology.

Like Da Vinci, Michelangelo may have been hiding ideas that would have got him in trouble with the Church.

BELOW

SISTINE SECRETS
Did Michelangelo hide a secret code, made up of mystical Jewish symbols that were intended to insult the Pope?

By now, Da Vinci scholars have scanned every inch of page 1033, trying to make sense of the prophecy and trying to figure out what the missing piece is. So the idea that this drawing may not only be a Da Vinci—but the missing piece and part of the prophecy—is huge. Also, considering that a cardinal believed something about this drawing was so important that he felt it needed to be carefully hidden, I want to know: What was history's greatest mind trying to tell us?

NO QUESTION, DA VINCI WAS A GENIUS—but a controversial one. In an age when Europeans were put to death for dissecting cadavers, he was the guy who secretly performed more than 30 human dissections. Why was he doing it? During Da Vinci's time, when anatomy was studied, the lessons taught were based upon ancient Greek and Roman texts, particularly those of Galen (130–200 CE) and his predecessor Hippocrates. Galen's knowledge and insights were 13 centuries old and astonishingly inaccurate, containing errors and misunderstandings of the workings of the body and even placement of the organs.

Further compounding the problem was the requirement that when dissection was available to medical students, they were examining animals, generally pigs.

To Da Vinci, that was ridiculous. Indeed, he was fascinated with the human anatomy. Using only the crude instruments of his day, he dissected and drew the different parts of the brain. He made major breakthroughs in our understandings of the backbone. In fact,

in 2005, Francis Wells developed a revolutionary technology to repair damaged hearts that was based on Da Vinci's diagrams from *500 years ago*. But despite the great advancements in medicine, the Church was opposed to dissecting cadavers.

Why?

In Italy in the 1400s, the Catholic Church was more powerful than the government. And the Church was deeply committed to protecting that power. Revolutionary ideas and insights into science could easily threaten the institution, and some were thus forbidden or suppressed.

Is that why Cardinal Tadini hid his part of page 1033 of the *Codex Atlanticus*? We asked that exact question to Father Norman Tanner in Italy. Could this self-portrait have contained hidden meanings or symbols?

"Throughout the medieval periods, there was a lot of interest in the occult and prophecy and so on," he told us. "So that was quite standard. And they also liked writing in secret language and so on. So that was part of life."

So did that mean the sketch could contain messages about the future?

"Yes . . . it's possible," Father Tanner added. "They rather liked this kind of playful hiding and a certain amount of secrecy within paintings. Yes, we find that in many other painters."

In the end, though, according to Father Tanner, the Church eventually embraced Da Vinci and much of his

DA VINCI AND COMIC BOOKS

Leonardo da Vinci's work also changed the course of comic books in the 20th century. When Bill Finger and Bob Kane were creating their new superhero in the 1930s, they looked at Da Vinci's design for his ornothopter flying device and took it as inspiration for the winged look of their character's cape. The character they were creating? None other than Batman. Without Da Vinci, there is no Batman.

TOP
CAPED CRUSADER
The wings of Da Vinci's ornothopter flying device was an acknowledged inspiration for the design of Batman's cape.

BOTTOM
A VISION OF FLYING
Da Vinci's bird-inspired design for his ornothopter flying device predated the Wright brothers by centuries.

work, even if they didn't entirely understand him. So the question remains: Why would Da Vinci place a self-portrait among his most cryptic prophecies? To find the answer, we needed to look at his other works.

INSIDE THE PAINTINGS

ACCORDING TO *MONA LISA* EXPERT Marina Wallace, Da Vinci's *Codex Atlanticus* contained "considerations about how one should behave, and how one should expect things to be. They're kind of ways of deep, deep thought, using very clever wording."

That wasn't the only place he hid certain meanings. During his life, Da Vinci thought a lot about the future, and we know he was obsessed with water. When he died, he was preparing what many believe would have been his last masterpiece. It was to be called *The Great Flood*.

The sketches show storms so violent, they topple mountains. There is great power in the sketches, but also great sadness; all of the enormous artistic talent and skill of Leonardo da Vinci are here,

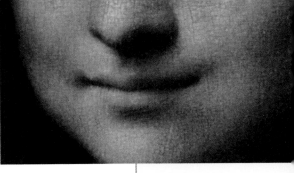

but also a weariness, perhaps even despair. Some experts told us they've spotted Da Vinci's own self-portrait in the art. We don't see it. But take a look for yourself. What would another mysterious self-portrait mean?

"When he describes the flood, the deluge, with incredible words, it's very descriptive, and it's very evocative," Wallace explains. "And the drawings are very detailed and they're very specific drawings, looking at the destruction that such a natural event could bring, so he was pointing to the fact that these are the things that our human nature is going to be subjected to during our lifetime. If you want to extend that to the lifetime of all the ones that come after us, certainly you can say that that is a warning to ourselves as part of nature."

But of all the details Wallace shared with us, the most intriguing was simply this: That when Da Vinci was traveling, "he took the *Mona Lisa* with him wherever he went." He liked to have it with him.

OK . . . this is where we call time-out.

We all know the *Mona Lisa*. This seemingly simple image is possibly the most widely recognized and studied piece of art in the history of the world. It's estimated to be worth more than $700 million. But. Could there be more to this painting than meets the eye? This isn't just the plot of a novel. Could the *Mona Lisa* be the key to crack a code that spans Da Vinci's life's work?

MONA LISA'S SMILE

It is a smile people have dissected for centuries. There are numerous explanations and speculations. Some say Mona Lisa's smile is a private joke between Da Vinci and those who viewed the painting; others argue that the smile is a way for Leonardo, known for his eccentric sense of humor, to "wink" at himself, a bit of sly self-mockery. Still others argue that the smile represents secret knowledge possessed only by its artist. Knowledge that would be dangerous to Da Vinci personally— knowledge that might well foretell an apocalypse.

In other words: prophetic knowledge.

"The genius of Leonardo is that he was able to put all that he learned inside his paintings, and put messages in there that speak to us over the ages." — SILVANO VINCETTI, ART HISTORIAN

THE MONA LISA

ACCORDING TO WALLACE, when you look closely at the *Mona Lisa,* there's actually water in the background of the painting—like a beautiful nature scene. But if you look even closer, the water is clearly higher on one side than the other, as though a flood is inevitable.

And here's the thing: If you pull Mona Lisa *out of the painting,* the waters come crashing together. The only thing stopping the flood is the figure, alleged by some to be a self-portrait.

So again we have to ask (and yes, it sounds crazy to me too, but . . .), could the *Mona Lisa* be part of a larger story—Da Vinci's story—of the end of the world?

When we asked the question of art historian Silvano Vincetti, he explained that in the left eye of Mona Lisa "there is the letter *S.* In the right eye there is the letter *L.* Then in the background of the painting, underneath the arch, there is the number *72.* During this period of the Renaissance, geometric symbols and numbers were very important."

How important? When you're investigating signs and symbols, the numbers *7* and *2* come up time and time again.

(In fact, I hide the number *27* in every single one of my novels.) But in Leonardo's case, many of the hidden codes are more personal. For reasons not fully understood, he was obsessed with the numbers *7* and *2*—as well as their combined forms of *27* and *72*—and hid them in many works, including his two most famous:

- A stone bridge in the *Mona Lisa*'s background contains the number *72*.

- There are 72 panels in the ceiling above the gathering at *The Last Supper*.

But there is more to 72 than the numbers *7* and *2*. And there is more to Leonardo's use of them than their presence in the *Mona Lisa* and *The Last Supper*. Among other things, Da Vinci:

- Designed a unique geometric shape that has 72 sides

- Designed his famous *Vitruvian Man* drawing around a basis of 27- and 72-degree angles

Why these numbers?

Because they have biblical connections. According to Vincetti, the number *27* refers to the Book of Revelation (the Book of Revelation is the 27th book in the New Testament) in which the author describes a series of violent events that were to occur at the end of the world.

The number *72* is also a biblical reference. It refers to the number of races that survived Noah's Ark. That's right: The number *72* doesn't

BELOW
VITRUVIAN MAN
Da Vinci designed his famous Vitruvian Man *drawing around a basis of 27- and 72-degree angles, which he also did in the* Mona Lisa *and* The Last Supper. *Those numbers keep showing up in his work.*

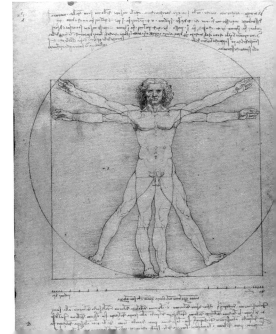

just relate to an apocalyptic story, but to a story describing a worldwide flood.

Notice a theme here? Prophecies. Apocalypse. The end of the world. In the *Mona Lisa*, we saw Da Vinci's potential warning about the power of nature and the dangers of floods. Even better, Da Vinci is known to have copied flood-related passages from the Bible and kept them in his workrooms and studios. In addition, remember what would've been Da Vinci's last great painting? *The Great Flood*.

According to Bruce Edelstein, a professor at NYU in Florence, "Leonardo not only made many drawings of

water and included the representation of water and aqueous bodies in many of his paintings, but he also wrote about water in the *Codex Atlanticus* itself. And they were talking about flooding, the dangers of flooding, and how conscious Leonardo would've been of that. One of the things that he wrote in the *Codex Atlanticus* was: 'The swollen rivers overflow and submerge the wide lowlands and its inhabitants.' This sounds like some great mystery, some great apocalyptic happening that Leonardo is foretelling."

Indeed, Vincetti added, "The genius of Leonardo is that he was able to put all that he learned inside his paintings, and put messages in there that speak to us over the ages."

OK, I can believe he put some hidden meanings in his art. And it's clear that Da Vinci had an obsession with water, tidal waves, and floods. But it still doesn't answer the key question that we asked about the so-called prophecy in the *Codex Atlanticus:* In his work, was Da Vinci *predicting* a specific event we can prepare for . . . or was he simply observing the cycles of nature?

DA VINCI AS PROPHET

MOST OF US WILL AGREE that Da Vinci was a genius. But was he using his art to actually make prophecies about the future? Some try to draw connections—and c'mon, have you been reading this chapter? It's easy to start threading things together when you start pulling apart his secrets—but in my mind, it wasn't until we met Da Vinci scholar Marco Levi that we found our real answer.

FACING PAGE TOP
PORTRAIT OF THE ARTIST AS A YOUNG MAN
The earliest known self-portrait of Da Vinci was lost until the mid-twentieth century . . .

FACING PAGE BOTTOM
MASTERPIECE REGAINED
. . . when it was found, then later confirmed as the long-missing piece from the apocalyptic page 1033 of the Codex Atlanticus.

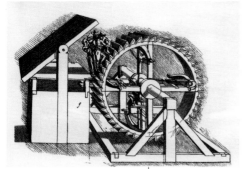

We asked Levi about Leonardo being a prophet. No question, he was a visionary, Levi agreed. But "if you ask me if he was able to predict what was going to happen . . . a certain disaster, on a certain day? No. He was a scientist who was trying to comprehend, to give an order to these things."

Exactly. A scientist.

"Like all the geniuses we had: Oppenheimer, Einstein, and others were not thinking to destroy the world," Levi pointed out. "They were thinking to give us something new . . . better for our future. So it depends how you use the things you have."

And right there is perhaps Da Vinci's most profound prediction of all.

Think back to those different interpretations of the *Mona Lisa*: She sits in the midst of nature. Just as *we* sit in the midst of nature. Will we sit there serenely as the female figure in the painting does? Or will we be crushed by nature's coming devastation?

It depends what you're looking for. And how you choose to act in this world.

During his lifetime, Da Vinci pursued innovations in medicine and engineering that improved health and quality of life. He also designed cutting-edge weapons to help us wage war. But when it comes to which we'll face — a calm peace or a riotous battle — the answer, so often, is simply . . . up to us.

That isn't just Da Vinci speaking to us from beyond the grave. As *Decoded* team member Buddy Levy pointed out, it's him speaking to us for all time.

CONCLUSION

WHAT SENT US DOWN THIS PATH was a new-found portrait by Leonardo da Vinci that came from his so-called book of prophecies. So what did the portrait mean? Was it a hint? A clue? A prophecy in itself? It was, because it's *Da Vinci himself* who's the answer.

It's Da Vinci himself who is absolute proof of the world's most beautiful secret: that the future is created *by us*, by human innovation. So what will the future bring? It depends how big we're willing to dream.

Almost 500 years ago, every single one of Da Vinci's inventions failed. The wings didn't help him fly. The scuba gear was made from a suit of leather. His pre-helicopter never took off. But over time, as human innovation caught up with his ideas, they all *worked*.

It is his ultimate prophecy: Be daring, be daring, always be daring.

There is no big dream unless you dream big.

IS THERE ANY GOLD IN FORT KNOX?

WHAT IF I TOLD YOU that Fort Knox is empty?

The last time anyone was allowed inside Fort Knox was in 1974, following a congressional call to see the gold.

Many experts today believe the soldiers stationed at Fort Knox are protecting absolutely *nothing*. They point to numerous theories to explain their beliefs.

Some say the gold was used to make off-the-books purchases. Others say it was used to manipulate the price of the dollar. And a few believe it was put to even darker uses. No one really knows.

But if you tell me that no one has been allowed to see our gold since 1974, I want to know if it's there. And I want to know what else is inside the vault.

That's why we went to Kentucky—to decode Fort Knox.

CHRISTINE

When I asked Senator Huddleston, "Do you think it's really empty?" he nodded and said, "Could be . . . could be."

When we walked out of the library together, he was moving slowly. I remembered then that he was in his eighties. Maybe he was slipping into a foggy haze of old age and wasn't remembering his facts correctly. As we approached the parking lot, I looked around to see who was here to pick up my confused and elderly friend. He then shook my hand, picked up the pace, and practically skipped over to his parked sedan. It occurred to me that he had been walking slowly because he was a gentleman and was waiting to open the door for me. He looked over his shoulder and asked, "Do you need a ride?"

"No, thank you," I said.

Senator Huddleston wasn't a kook at all. He wasn't foggy or confused. He was a perfectly sane man with the confidence to look me in the eye and clearly state, on the record, that Fort Knox could be empty.

ON APRIL 5, 1933—only one month and one day after being sworn in for his first term—President Franklin Delano Roosevelt issued Executive Order 6012, and with his signature made it illegal for private citizens to own gold. Roosevelt cited the crisis from the Great Depression as his reason.

To house all this gold, the U.S. Treasury built the vault at Fort Knox. It soon held more than half the world's known gold, worth some $200 billion.

The Kentucky location was chosen because it was landlocked, making it less susceptible to enemy attack. Today, Knox remains the most impregnable vault in the world, with a thousand miles of U.S. territory in every direction, and an enormous arsenal to protect it. To top it off, the granite foundation is five feet thick . . . and the vault door weighs some two and a half tons.

The price of gold has fluctuated wildly throughout the years — yet the government says that the value of our gold reserves has been almost exactly the same.

But how drastic and dramatic was the action to take gold from the American people?

Private ownership of gold became not just illegal but also punishable with stiff fines and jail terms of up to a decade.

While some citizens transferred their gold holdings to banks in Switzerland or other nations, most of the U.S. gold left private hands. Other than small amounts used in dentistry and jewelry, valuable coins held by collectors, and the five ounces that private citizens were still allowed to own, thousands of tons of gold were transferred to the government.

FDR
On April 5, 1933, because of the Great Depression, President Franklin Delano Roosevelt issued Executive Order 6012. From there, it became illegal for private citizens to own gold.

LEFT
THE CRASH
The collapse of the stock market in October 1929 caused the U.S. economy to grind to a halt, putting millions out of work and on the breadlines.

WHAT'S IN THERE?

SO LET'S ASK THE QUESTION: What's really inside Fort Knox?

Lawyer and journalist David Ganz was there the last time the depository was opened for inspection.

What Ganz saw is *exactly* what most of us would expect to see. "It was utterly amazing, one of the most exciting events I've ever been to," he said. "First, you're blinded by the light. The room was lined on three sides with gold, floor to ceiling. The second thing is a big, overwhelming sense of claustrophobia because of how small the room was."

Wait. *"Small?"* All of our gold is kept in a *small* room?

"It is a vault that is about eight or nine feet by ten feet high and fifteen feet deep," Ganz continued. But when we asked him if the vault could be empty, we were surprised to hear: "It's absolutely possible," Ganz replied. "The government could've done it. The only way that anybody is going to find out is to go back to Fort Knox and to look inside the vaults."

Indeed, unless the vault is opened for inspection, there's no way of knowing.

And now you're seeing the problem. Right now—today—there is *no* regular schedule for inspecting our

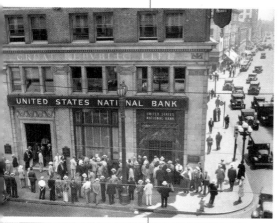

gold reserves. No public accounting or anything to produce *evidence* that the gold is still there.

"The Treasury Department is required to put out on a monthly basis an asset balance sheet of the U.S. government. I looked at that balance sheet, and it hasn't changed fifteen cents," Ganz explained.

But what makes that so concerning is the fact that the price of gold has fluctuated *wildly* throughout the years — yet the government says that the value of our gold reserves has been almost *exactly the same.*

To go further, let's stop for a quick economic primer: America's economy used to be based on the gold standard, which meant that dollar bills were really only deeds for a tiny portion of the nation's gold. That changed in 1971, when the government moved to a confidence-based economy. That means that for decades, we've relied on the principle of supply and demand, not the dollar's relationship to gold, to set the dollar's value.

And since the government controls the supply of gold, it has far more power to control the value of the dollar.

You top that off with the fact that there are no public audits, and my nose starts twitching. So what happens if Fort Knox is empty?

Think back to the national threat that caused Fort Knox to be opened: the Great Depression. The stock market had collapsed. The economy had ground to a halt. A quarter of the nation was without work. Factories were closed, stores were shuttered . . . and lines for soup kitchens and breadlines stretched down the block in every town.

ABOVE
FORT KNOX
The United States Bullion Depository at Fort Knox was built in 1936 to store a large portion of official U.S. gold reserves and other precious items. You won't believe what else was in there.

BELOW
GOOD LUCK GETTING IN
—or getting out, if you do. Among other things, Fort Knox boasts five-foot-thick granite walls and a blast-proof vault door. They can also flood it full of water so no one gets out.

THINKING ABOUT BREAKING INTO FORT KNOX?

The vault at Fort Knox is strong enough to withstand an actual nuclear blast.

When it was built, the vault door alone was a marvel of engineering. The closed vault is sealed with wax and tape designed to reveal even the slightest breach. And the depository's location itself plays a large role in safeguarding the gold.

Fort Knox is landlocked, which rules out both amphibious assault and, more importantly, amphibious *escape*. So if you're going to take the gold *out* of Fort Knox, you're going to have to do it by land or air. And think about this: Just moving the gold into the depository required 500 railroad cars.

Today, with more than 4,500 *tons* of gold supposedly stored in Fort Knox, it's estimated that flying the gold out would require 150 fully loaded 747s.

And don't forget that the depository itself is located on a major military base. I went there myself. In addition to the installation's sniper and machine gun towers— and the armed Apache helicopters—the installation is ringed with the highest tech fences and electronic surveillance you've ever seen. When we sent Buddy, McKinley, and Scott there, an unmarked black SUV

> **"Both the vault door and emergency door were 21 inches thick and made of the latest torch- and drill-resistant material. The main vault door weighed 20 tons and the vault casing was 25 inches thick."**
>
> —The Mosler Safe Company

showed up behind them within a few minutes.

Plus, even if you did get past the defenses, just opening that vault door requires ten separate people performing ten separate precise tasks.

Oh, and did I mention you probably need to bring some scuba gear? There's a rumor—neither confirmed nor denied by the government—that in the

event of a severe security breach, the vaults at Fort Knox could actually be flooded, drowning any intruders.

So it makes a bit more sense why supervillain Auric Goldfinger, from the James Bond classic, didn't set out to *steal* the gold from Fort Knox, but instead tried to destroy it with a nuke. (P.S. That vast, multilevel space where James Bond battled Goldfinger's deadly henchman Oddjob? That was a creation of set designer Ken Adam's imagination and had no reflection of reality.)

So who would have a chance of removing the gold from Fort Knox? Who else? The U.S. government itself.

THE HARD FACTS

Want to take a look at the Bullion Depository yourself? Here's what you'll be facing. According to the U.S. Mint, the gold is protected by:

- 16,000 cubic feet of granite
- 4,200 cubic yards of concrete
- 750 tons of reinforcing steel
- 670 tons of structural steel

Those materials were combined to produce a structure that boasts:

- Five-foot-thick granite walls
- Blast-proof vault door

Those same towns had seen many of their banks fail when depositors rushed to withdraw their savings — withdrawals that vastly exceeded the amounts of cash the banks had on hand.

To most people, *that* was far more terrifying than a plummeting stock market whose losses wiped out the millionaires. Imagine that *you* went to *your* bank and found it boarded up, your life's savings vanished. How would you react?

Anger, right? Followed quickly by fear. Then comes the panic.

It wouldn't be much different today. In our *confidence-based economy,* when you take away the confidence, well . . .

According to Ganz, there'd be "panic in the streets. You could have riots, you could have financial meltdown, and you could have people taking dollar bills and tearing them up and throwing them up in the air."

OK, that might be a bit dramatic, but Ganz is making a vital point about *hyperinflation,* which is what happens when money literally becomes not worth the paper it's printed on.

It happens all the time . . . the Germans saw it in 1923, when firewood cost 850 billion marks. Greece experienced it in 1943, when milk went to 2 million drachmas a liter. And it happened in Brazil in 1993, when a bottle of suntan lotion cost 800,000 cruzeiros reais.

Needless to say, the way the world's economies are interconnected, there'd be the potential for a global financial meltdown. And that's definitely at least one motive for why the government wouldn't want you knowing if the Fort Knox gold was gone.

ABOVE
ONE LAST LOOK
Mary Brooks, director of the Mint, led the last inspection of Fort Knox in September 1974. That means the last time anyone was in there, the Jackson 5 were just getting started.

THE SPECS

NO CIVILIAN HAS BEEN ALLOWED TO SEE THE GOLD in Fort Knox since 1974. As for the vault itself, it doesn't require an enormous amount of space. According to the U.S. Mint, each of the standard gold bars present fits the following specifications:

- Size of a standard gold bar: 7 inches x 3⅝ inches x 1¾ inches

- Weight of a standard gold bar: approximately 400 ounces or 27.5 pounds

To accommodate the 4,500 tons, you'd need 33,000 or so gold bars. Admittedly, that's a lot of gold bars, but you wouldn't need the Grand Canyon to store them. The vault at Fort Knox held them comfortably.

After the 1974 inspection, the vault was closed, the seals replaced, and no member of the public has seen the interior of the vault since.

Not that there haven't been plenty of requests.

All of which have been denied.

Why deny letting people inside? Isn't it, after all, *our* gold? Why *shouldn't* designated representatives from Congress or the press be allowed to see it? The official responses are the same as they've been throughout the history:

- TRADITION: The Mint releases a listing of regular assets—but audits and viewings have *never* been frequent. Indeed, just months before the 1974 public audit,

Mint director Mary Brooks summed up the Mint's position in this simple statement: "The policy against visitors is long-standing."

- COST: Expense has been used as a rationale for keeping the vault closed. Federal officials have claimed that a true audit—including drilling into the gold to check its level of purity—could cost tens of millions of dollars.

- YOUR GOLD IS NONE OF YOUR BUSINESS: This is the most frequent reason for refusal.

Since 1967, the Freedom of Information Act (FOIA) has permitted citizens to formally request federal documents and other information. The government is required to comply with the request—unless the request runs into one of FOIA's numerous exceptions.

So is Fort Knox an exception to FOIA? Of course it is. The contents of Fort Knox are considered *classified material.*

But wait, it gets better. Check out this 1976 addition to the list of exceptions to FOIA: "related to information which would lead to financial speculation or endanger the stability of any financial institution." FOIA isn't likely to get past that one.

INSIDE THE ACTOR'S STUDIO

IF THE GOAL WAS TO FIND OUT WHAT'S IN THE VAULT, there was only one place to make that happen: We headed to Fort Knox.

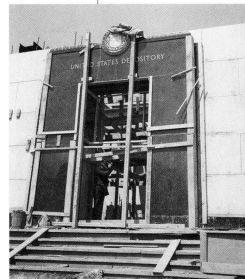

BELOW
AN IMPREGNABLE FORTRESS
Under construction in 1936, the plan was that there would be no more secure spot in America—and possibly on Earth—than Fort Knox.

"We were told to issue no ammunition. And because I was a returning vet, I questioned it. And the officer in charge was a friend of mine. He pulled me aside and said we don't issue weapons with ammunition simply because there is no gold in Fort Knox."

— CRAIG HULET, STATIONED AT FORT KNOX

Of course, as I mentioned before, there was no way we were getting inside.

Still, even if we couldn't get in, that doesn't mean there aren't others with eyes and ears inside there. One such person was Craig Hulet, who told us, "I was stationed at Fort Knox after I returned from Vietnam. I was a senior armor, and I issued weapons to those people that guarded Fort Knox."

Perfect person to speak to, right? We thought so, too. Especially when we heard Hulet's real bombshell: "We were told to issue no ammunition. And because I was a returning vet, I questioned it. And the officer in charge was a friend of mine. He pulled me aside and said we don't issue weapons with ammunition simply because there is no gold in Fort Knox."

Read that line again: "There is no gold in Fort Knox."

It's one thing for a lower guard like Hulet to say that. But even Hulet asked his superior what was going on. His captain's response? "He said that he understood that there

was no gold," Hulet added. "And he did give me a reason why because I thought, *Well then, this is foolish. What are we doing?* There's people that are going to come to Fort Knox. Let's assume they believe there's gold. They're going to come armed. So either way, we're stuck with no ammunition. These people believe there's gold. He said it's simple: We let them in and we zip it up."

Zip it up?

"In other words, they disappear."

So does Hulet think the government will ever come clean about the gold being gone?

"No. They don't tell us anything unless they're absolutely forced to. This isn't a crime. That's what's most important to me to understand it. When you realize that this is a policy of the government. This is not theft, this is not . . . it's not crooks and liars. We're not going to catch anybody and put anybody in jail. What we're going to find is that we've got a policy in place still to this day that says we're not going to be on a gold standard. And now we can never be on a gold standard. There's not sufficient gold. . . . Your children, grandchildren, your future. You've been robbed."

We heard the same from a local waitress whose mother was in the military and guarded the gold vault. Did her mom ever mention what was inside Fort Knox? "She said no, there's no gold in the gold vault." She went on to say, "There used to be gold in the gold vault. There's nothing left but dust. And everybody around here pretty much knows that there's no gold in the gold vault."

Worst of all, Craig Hulet and that waitress aren't the only ones who think that.

ABOVE

MILTARY BASE

How well protected is the gold? The Depository is located on a major military base. In addition to the installation's sniper and machine gun towers—and armed Apache helicopters—it is ringed with high-tech fences and electronic surveillance. No question, the gold is safe . . . if the gold is in there.

RON PAUL

Most people know Ron Paul as a presidential candidate from Texas. But the congressman has long been a loud advocate for a new audit of Fort Knox.

When we tracked him down, we reached out to him with some questions . . . and the 21-year veteran of the House of Representatives got right back to us. But rather than simply tell you what he said, look at Exhibit 3A (facing page), and you'll find the actual transcript of his answers.

In the end, Ron Paul offered powerful words from an elected official . . . telling us that the public is potentially being duped about the contents of Fort Knox. And the deeper we dug, we kept finding similar sentiments.

THEN WHAT WAS IT USED FOR?

ONE OF THE BEST PEOPLE TO ANSWER THAT QUESTION was former Kentucky senator Walter "Dee" Huddleston, who also agreed to speak with us.

Beyond being the former senator from the state that actually houses Fort Knox, Senator Huddleston had one other major claim to gold fame: He was one of the few people that they allowed in Fort Knox when it was audited back in 1974.

Y'see, back then, there was a similar uproar by people who wanted to see the gold.

According to Senator Huddleston, "People had reported that they had seen shipments of gold going out of there and perhaps going to a foreign country or something. I guess we're engaged in activities that are secret. And activities that are believed to be in our best interest and protecting us some. And for those kinds of situations, yeah, I think it should be used, if you want to use it, without publication."

But did that mean that some of the gold could've been used—whether to protect us or pay off an enemy?

"I would say it's possible, yes," Senator Huddleston said. "But as far as the money and the gold, I don't see any reason why the American public shouldn't know what we've got up there. It's ours."

So what if we find out it's half empty?

"I think [it] would be a terrible shock to many people in the country," the senator replied. "And the whole economy might go under."

So what would Senator Huddleston do then?

"I don't know. Run for the border."

THE MAN INSIDE

BETWEEN 1975 AND 1986, Doug Simmons was a stack foreman at Fort Knox. That means he stacked gold in the actual vault. He saw at least some of the gold there—and was the one who told us what else the government had stored inside in the past (see page 154). But when asked what else could be stored inside Fort Knox today, Simmons told us to "look at the growing array of security that continues to go around that vault, year after year. All the locals know: more fencing, more cameras, more presence of guards. Humvees going around the building on a regular basis . . . people up on the rooftops and stuff. Things you didn't see so much back in the 1970s, when there was one wrought-iron fence around the building. This is vastly changed since 9/11. If you go onto that property and you don't stop, they're going to kill you."

A few years ago, I was invited to speak at Fort Knox, and a colonel there rewarded me with this U.S. Army Challenge Coin for excellence.

1 DECODED:
2   Do the American people have a right to know
3   what's in their Treasury?
4 RON PAUL:
5   Of course they do, the gold was originally
6   stolen from the American people by the gov-
7   ernment in the 1930s, so they have a right to
8   know if the government still holds it.
9 DECODED:
10   What is the main reason the government op-
11   erates in such secrecy with regard to Fort
12   Knox's holdings?
13 RON PAUL:
14   The government always operates in secrecy on
15   everything. There is nothing too unimportant
16   to be classified if the government feels like
17   it. The government feels like it is our bet-
18   ter, and treats the people the same way a par-
19   ent would treat a little child.
20 DECODED:
21   Do you think Fort Knox could be empty?
22 RON PAUL:
23   It is certainly possible, I haven't seen the
24   gold myself, and I don't believe that any Con-
25   gressman has since the 1970s. I don't think
26   it's likely, though. What a lot of people are
27   more concerned about is whether any of this
28   gold is involved in gold lending or gold swaps
29   with bullion banks, foreign governments, cen-
30   tral banks, etc.
31 DECODED:
33   Is gold an important national resource, and
34   what would the implications be if the gold re-
35   sources were depleted?
36 RON PAUL:
37   The government obviously feels that it is,
38   otherwise it wouldn't continue to hold 8000
39   tons of it. It's funny how on the one hand
40   they denigrate gold as a "barbarous relic" and
41   downplay the importance of gold as currency,
42   yet on the other hand they don't want to get
43   rid of any of it. Since it was taken from the
44   American people almost 80 years ago, it really
45   ought to be returned to them. Just sell it
46   back to them.

IF THERE'S NO GOLD, WHAT'S INSIDE IT?

Fort Knox is famous for its gold vault, but throughout history, at different times, it's also held our nation's most vital items. Among the items the government has stored there:

- In the 1940s, it held the Magna Carta, which we held for the British to keep it out of the hands of the Nazis.

- The vault also held the Declaration of Independence, the Constitution, the Gettysburg Address, and three copies of the Gutenberg Bible.

- In the 1950s, the vault became part of the Cold War era and held drugs, vaccines, and morphine in case of mass casualties.

As a result of the friendship we struck—and that I very much respect—he tried to make us the first civilians to get access to the vault since 1974. But even with all that pull, the real boss—the Treasury Department—still wouldn't let us near it. Yes, we found the answer of what else was in there besides gold. But is the gold itself gone?

According to the *Times* of London, not even the auditors who prepare the annual inventory of assets are allowed to look inside the vault at Fort Knox.

We just have to take the government's word that the gold is all there.

It's called . . . *confidence.*

Does that mean there'd be a full economic collapse if it was revealed there was no gold inside?

Depends who you ask. But know this: The gold inside Fort Knox is a *symbol* as much as it is an asset—and once that symbol is destroyed, the confidence the symbol represents goes with it.

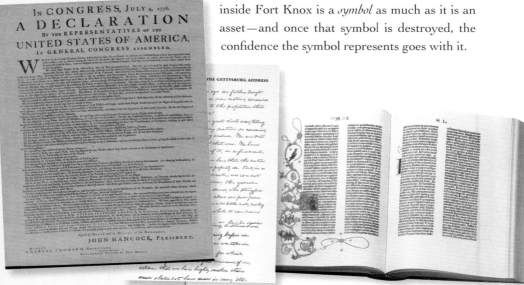

SOME FINAL THOUGHTS

PEOPLE READ *THE WIZARD OF OZ*—written in 1900—as a children's fantasy. But to others, it's actually a story about gold:

A country kid from the Midwest loses her house—teams up with a farmer and an industrial worker—and battles wicked forces from the West to the East.

The only way to save herself is to follow the Yellow Brick Road, *which sure looks like gold to me.*

And by the way, what is gold measured in? Ounces, or *O-Z*. Get it?

When she gets to Oz, what does Dorothy find behind it all? A corrupt politician behind the curtains, pulling strings and controlling the little people.

Today, our entire monetary system is based on trust. But for nearly 50 years, it's had to be blind trust. The gold belongs to Americans . . . and Americans pay to protect it. However, we'll never truly know what we have until Fort Knox finally opens its doors once more.

That's the reason this chapter made the book. There's nothing I believe in more than the power of an ordinary person. If you want to see Fort Knox opened, ask for it.

And watch what happens.

FACING PAGE
WHAT ELSE IS IN THERE?
The Gutenberg Bible, the Gettysburg Address, and the Declaration of Independence have all been stored in Fort Knox at one time or another.

Aliens landed here

Roswell Daily Record

ROSWELL, NEW MEXICO, TUESDAY, JULY 8, 1947

RECORD PHONES
Business Office 2288
News Department 2287

5c PER COPY.

Claims Army Is Stacking Courts Martial

Indiana Senator Lays Protest Before Patterson

Washington, July 8 (UP)—Senator Jenner (R-Ind.) contended today that "the high command in the European theatre is stacking courts martial against defendants in court martial.

In a letter to Secretary of War Patterson demanding a full investigation of army military trial procedure, Jenner offered what he said was documentary proof...

RAAF Captures Flying Saucer On Ranch in Roswell Region

House Passes Tax Slash by Large Margin

Defeat Amendment By Demos to Remove — Rolls

Security Council Paves Way to Talks On Arms Reductions

Lake Success, July 8 (UP)—The United Nations security council today approved an American blueprint for arms reduction discussions despite a Russian warning that the plan would bring about a collapse of arms regulation efforts.

No Details of Flying Disk Are Revealed

Roswell Hardware Man and Wife Report Disk Seen

The intelligence office of the 509th Bombardment group at Roswell Army Air Field announced at noon today, that the field has...

Ex-King Carol Weds Mme. Lupescu

<del>CONFIDENTIAL</del>
UNCLASSIFIED

SECURITY INFORMATION

STATUS REPORT

PROJECT BLUE BOOK - REPORT NO. 8

FORMERLY PROJECT GRUDGE

PROJECT NO. 10073
31 DECEMBER 1952

DECLASSIFIED
Authority NND 752057
By _____ NARA Date 1/1/

AIR TECHNICAL INTELLIGENCE CENTER
WRIGHT-PATTERSON AIR FORCE BASE
OHIO

UFOS:
INSIDE ROSWELL AND AREA 51

WHAT IF I TOLD YOU that our government is hiding definitive proof of the existence of alien life?

Would you even be surprised? According to a recent poll, more than 40 million Americans claim to have seen, or know someone who claims to have seen, an Unidentified Flying Object, or UFO. Among those people: U.S. Presidents Jimmy Carter and Ronald Reagan and countless civilian and military pilots.

Yet the government, including both political and military leaders, continues to maintain that it has no official knowledge or evidence of extraterrestrial life.

Is the government lying—and if so, why?

Of all the things you've emailed me about, here's one of the most requested: It's time to decode what the government knows about alien life.

UFOs. Flying saucers.

Everybody's heard of them — and everybody has an opinion about whether or not they provide evidence of extraterrestrial life.

But nobody, at least according to the most official sources, has any hard evidence that aliens have visited our skies or landed on the earth, despite more than 60 years of stories, reports, photographs, testimonies, and wide-ranging government investigations.

With that long a time line, and that many different threads to pull together, you might think it's hard to know where to begin. It's not. Because we all know there's really only one place to start: the site of the most famous alleged UFO incident of all time. Roswell, New Mexico.

ROSWELL

HERE'S WHAT MOST PEOPLE KNOW ABOUT ROSWELL, NEW MEXICO. In July 1947, a public information officer issued a press release saying they recovered a *flying disc*. This has come to be known as the "Roswell Incident," or the "Roswell Crash."

But the first real sighting of a UFO — and the incident that gave "flying saucers" their name — had occurred a month earlier, half a continent away.

On June 24, 1947, a businessman and private pilot named Kenneth Arnold was piloting his airplane near Mount Rainier, Washington, when he saw . . . something.

Actually, he claimed to have seen *several* somethings. According to Arnold's report (see Exhibit 2A, page 160), he spotted a group of nine glowing objects flying in a V-formation, traveling at speeds he estimated to be 1,700 mph. At the time, we had not yet broken the sound barrier, a feat that required achieving a speed of at least 768 mph, so what Arnold saw was moving nearly 1,000 mph *faster* than we'd ever moved.

In addition, these weren't typical aircraft with a wings-fuselage-tail structure. Arnold described the flying objects as "disc-shaped," comparing their movements to the skipping of a saucer across water. The press seized on that last image, and the label "flying saucers" was born.

It's hard to think of a more famous label—or a more controversial one. Initial reaction from the few officials who looked into the sighting dismissed Arnold's report as a publicity stunt. But that accusation wouldn't stick. Kenneth Arnold was an experienced pilot with more than 9,000 total flying hours—and not the sort of man who made up a wild tale just to garner attention. If he saw something, there was something to see.

Within a matter of weeks, though, the Arnold sighting was eclipsed by the most famous of all. You know the one: Roswell.

Unlike the Arnold sighting—where the UFOs were observed, then flew away—the Roswell incident involved a UFO that was actually on the ground. Some say it crashed on the nearby Foster Ranch, others that the craft had landed. Either way, there was finally some hard evidence, gathered at the site, rather than just

BELOW
RANCH
WRECKAGE
Brig. General Roger M. Ramey and Col. Thomas J. Dubose, 8th Air Force Chief of Staff, identify metallic fragments found by a farmer near Roswell. Those pieces were later claimed to be a weather balloon.

UFO SIGHTING
MT RANIER, WASHINGTON
24 June 1947

On 24 June 1947 at 1400 Mr. Kenneth Arnold took off from the Chehalis, Washington Airport in his personal plane and headed for Yakima, Washington. Mr. Arnold's trip was delayed for an hour in search of a large marine transport that supposedly went down near or around the southwest side of Mt. Ranier. After take-off Mr. Arnold flew directly toward Mt. Ranier at an altitude of approximately 9,500 feet, which is the approximate elevation of the high plateau from which Mt. Ranier rises. He made one sweep of this high plateau to the westward, searching all of the various ridges for the marine ship and flew to the west near the ridge side of the canyon where Ashford, Washington is located. Unable to see anything that looked like the lost plane, Mr. Arnold made a 360 degree turn to the right above the town of Mineral, starting again toward Mt. Ranier and climbing to an altitude of 9,200 feet.

Mr. Arnold reported that the air was so smooth that it was a real pleasure flying, and, as most pilots do when the air is smooth and they are at a higher altitude, he trimmed out the aircraft and simply sat in his plane observing the sky and terrain.

Mr. Arnold reported that there was a DC-4 to his left and rear at approximately 14,000 feet. The sky was reported to be as clear as crystal. He hadn't flown more than two or three minutes on his course when a bright flash reflected on his airplane. He couldn't find where the reflection came from, but to the left and north of Mt. Ranier he did observe a chain of nine peculiar looking objects flying from north to south at approximately 9,500 feet. They were approaching Mt. Ranier very rapidly, and he assumed that they were jet aircraft. Every few seconds two or three of the objects would dip or change course slightly, just enough for the sun to strike them at an angle and reflect brightly. The objects being quite far away, he was unable to make out their shape or formation. As they approached Mt. Ranier he observed their outline quite clearly. Mr. Arnold stated that he found it very peculiar that he couldn't find their tails but assumed they were some type of jet aircraft. The objects were observed to pass the southern edge of Mt. Ranier flying directly south to south-east down the hog's back of a mountain range. The elevation of the objects was estimated to have varied approximately one thousand feet one way or another but remained very near the horizon, which would indicate that they were near the same elevation as the witness. Mr. Arnold stated that the objects flew like geese, in a rather diagonal chain-like line as if they were linked together. They seemed to hold a definite direction but swerved in and out of the high mountain peaks. The witness estimated the distance between him and the objects to be approximately 25 miles. Using a Zeus fastener, or cowling tool, he estimated the size of the objects to be approximately two thirds that of a DC-4. He observed the UFO's passing a high snow covered ridge in between Mt. Ranier and Mt. Adams and reported that as the first object was passing the south crest of this ridge the last one was entering the northern crest of the ridge. Later measurement of length of this particular ridge revealed it was approximately five miles, so it was estimated the chain of objects was five miles long. Mr. Arnold timed the objects between Mt. Ranier and Mt. Adams and determined they crossed this 47 miles in one minute and forty-two seconds. This is equivilant to 1656.71 miles per hour.

In a subsequent interview Mr. Arnold described the objects as appearing like saucers skipping on water. This description was shortened to "Flying Saucers" by newspaper men and resulted in the popular use of this term.

It is the Air Force conclusion that the objects of this sighting were due to a mirage. Mr. Arnold's statement concerning how smooth and crystal clear the air was is an indication of very stable conditions which are associated with inversions, and increase the refraction index of the atmosphere.

"The many rumors regarding the flying disc became a reality yesterday when the intelligence office of the 509th Bomb Group of the Eighth Air Force, Roswell Army Air Field, was fortunate enough to gain possession of a disc through the cooperation of one of the local ranchers and the sheriff's office. . . . Action was immediately taken and the disc was picked up at the rancher's home. It was inspected at the Roswell Army Air Field and subsequently loaned by Major Marcel to higher headquarters." —ORIGINAL ROSWELL PRESS RELEASE

some vague description of what someone saw in the air from a distance.

Right there, a U.S. Army public information officer issued a press release saying they recovered a flying disc. The very next day, the military retracted that statement and said it was a radar-tracking balloon, not a flying saucer.

So what happened?

Let's start with the incident itself.

First of all, it didn't start at the Roswell Army Air Field. It began just north when, at some point in late June or early July 1947, something crashed on the nearby Foster Ranch. The ranch foreman said that he found unusual materials on the Foster land and reported those findings to the Chaves County sheriff. The sheriff, in turn, passed the word to officials at the Roswell Army Air Field, which on July 7, 1947, dispatched a team to investigate and bring back evidence.

FACING PAGE
EXHIBIT 2A
Pilot Kenneth Arnold's Report.

BELOW
**A NATIONAL
OBSESSION**
*Reports of mysterious
sightings increased
rapidly after the Roswell
incident. Was there
an actual increase
in UFOs — or only
an increase in public
fascination with them?*

So again . . . what happened?

For answers, we started by talking to Julie Shuster, the director of the International UFO Museum and Research Center. But what makes Shuster even more interesting is that her father was Lieutenant Walter Haut, the Roswell public information officer who issued the original press release. (Exhibit 2B, facing page, is part of the original redacted government press release that was actually issued at Roswell.)

According to Shuster, "On July 8, 1947, Colonel Blanchard called him in that morning and said you need to issue a press release, we found a flying saucer. So he issued a press release. Basically: *We have in our possession a flying saucer. It's being flown to higher headquarters.*"

But according to Shuster, "There was a contradictory story the next day . . . from General Ramey, saying basically, *It's a weather balloon. People here didn't know what they were talking about.* And once they said it's a weather balloon, it's classified. *Done.*"

Indeed, within a single day, Lieutenant Haut's press release was being denied by the head of the Air Force himself, General Roger M. Ramey. Instead of a flying disc of unknown origin, the debris collected from the New Mexico ranch was the remains of a standard weather balloon that military bases launched frequently to measure atmospheric conditions.

And there's the key question, right? Maybe it *was* just a weather balloon. But before you decide,

'Fireball' Flashes Across NM Skies, Explodes in Hills

SANTA FE, March 7 (UP)—A University of New Mexico professor today trailed a brilliant "fireball" which flashed across the skies of northeastern New Mexico, then apparently exploded with a deafening roar in the Chico Hills of Colfax and Mora Counties.

Dr. Lincoln La Paz, UNM, meteoritics expert, told United Press he had received reports on the ball itself from Albuquerque, East Las Vegas, Clayton, Roswell and Santa Fe.

State Police Capt. Pen. Winston of Springer said residents of Roy reported an explosion which rattled windows about 2:30 yesterday afternoon. In Roy newspaperman Karl Guthman said "We are pretty much concerned about it here."

WHITE SANDS PROVING GROUNDS, March 7 (UP)—A spokesman at this rocket testing area said today that no rockets were fired from the area yesterday.

His statement was in answer to questions about the mysterious fire-ball that streaked across the skies yesterday afternoon and thundered to the earth somewhere in the northeastern portion of the state.

He said the explosion was ap-

said it had a tail like a jet, only it was a staggered affair.

From Raton Dr. W. L. Hatcher, veterinarian, and his assistant, Tony Schuster, said they were at the Jack Davenport ranch east of Farley at 2:30.

Schuster said he saw vapor in the air like a jet plane and heard a sound like thunder.

He said he was tempted to hit the dirt, and thought it might be a buzz bomb.

He said he saw an object in the sky, about the size of a milk bottle, traveling so fast it was out of sight in a second.

Dr. LaPaz started immediately for the area in an effort to "get my hands on one of the things and find out what it is." He has been chasing similar reports for more than two years.

"It must have been incredibly brilliant to have been seen in yesterday's bright sunlight," the enthusiastic professor declared.

LaPaz said the object was first

Roswell
(1 page)

TELETYPE

FBI DALLAS   7-8-47   6-17 PM

DIRECTOR AND SAC, CINCINNATI   URGENT

FLYING DISC, INFORMATION CONCERNING.   HEADQUARTERS

EIGHTH AIR FORCE, TELEPHONICALLY ADVISED THIS OFFICE THAT AN OBJECT
PURPORTING TO BE A FLYING DISC WAS RE COVERED NEAR ROSWELL, NEW
MEXICO, THIS DATE. THE DISC IS HEXAGONAL IN SHAPE AND WAS SUSPENDED
FROM A BALLON BY CABLE, WHICH BALLON WAS APPROXIMATELY TWENTY
FEET IN DIAMETER. _____ FURTHER ADVISED THAT THE OBJECT
FOUND RESEMBLES A HIGH ALTITUDE WEATHER BALLOON WITH A RADAR
REFLECTOR, BUT THAT TELEPHONIC CONVERSATION BETWEEN THEIR OFFICE
AND WRIGHT FIELD HAD NOT _____ BORNE OUT THIS BELIEF. DISC AND
BALLOON BEING TRANSPORTED TO WRIGHT FIELD BY SPECIAL PLANE FOR EXAMINATI
INFORMATION PROVIDED THIS OFFICE BECAUSE OF NATIONAL INTEREST IN CASE
XXXX AND FACT THAT NATIONAL BROADCASTING COMPANY, ASSOCIATED PRESS, AND
OTHERS ATTEMPTING TO BREAK STORY OF LOCATION OF DISC TODAY. _____
_____ ADVISED WOULD REQUEST WRIGHT FIELD TO ADVISE CINCINNATI
OFFICE RESULTS OF EXAMINATION. NO FURTHER INVESTIGATION BEING
CONDUCTED.

WYLY
END   RECORDED

CXXXX ACK IN ORDER   EX-29   23 JUL 22 1947

UA 92 FBI CI MJW

BPI H8

8-38 PM O

6-22 PM OK FBI WASH D

OK FBI CI MJ

here's one fact that you need to know: At the time of the Roswell sighting, weather balloons were made from a flexible, lightweight neoprene rubber, weighing in at less than a single pound. Tethered to the train of the balloon would be a short nylon kite-tail featuring a data transmitter. But that's about as complicated as these devices got. Lieutenant Haut described something *otherworldly* and *indestructible*. So ask yourself this: Could an accomplished military man and aviator really confuse an extraterrestrial spacecraft . . . with a one-pound weather balloon?

The answer didn't really matter, because once the general said it was a weather balloon . . . that became the official story of Roswell. And to make sure that the official version wasn't questioned, the pieces of the weather balloon were classified.

Why's a weather balloon suddenly *classified*? Apparently, this wasn't a run-of-the-mill weather balloon, but an *advanced* balloon used for surveillance. Walter Haut's daughter, Julie Shuster, is one of the doubters, and she's made her skepticism very clear.

According to Shuster, her father actually handled the debris that was recovered from the ranch. And he not only

BELOW
MYSTERIOUS FORMS
The Air Force insisted that sightings of body bags used to recover alien crash victims were in fact test dummies placed inside insulation bags to protect sensitive equipment.

handled it, but he reported that it couldn't be cut, torn, or burned. It was unlike any material Haut—or anyone else on Earth—had ever seen.

Years after the incident, Haut revealed something else to his daughter: The disc that was recovered from the Foster ranch was approximately 22 feet in diameter, far larger than a weather balloon. Large enough to carry passengers.

"My father saw something under a tarp at the hangar," she says. And did he describe it? "Large black eyes. Slits for nose. Little slit for mouth. Slits for ears," Shuster added. "Long extended four fingers, longer arms, which to me is pretty detailed for somebody that didn't see something."

Pretty detailed for sure. But you want to know the most vital part of the story? Roswell Army Air Field was the home base for the 509th Bombardment Wing. Know what they were responsible for? Dropping the atomic bombs on Japan two years earlier.

"These were not typical GIs," said engineer Dennis Balthaser, a Roswell resident and longtime investigator of UFOs. "These were the best we had. The best pilots, the best navigators—and to say that they could handle and deliver the atomic bomb, but were too dumb to know the difference between a weather balloon and a flying saucer is not something I can buy into."

Moreover, Balthaser knew and respected Walter Haut, adding that Haut told him as well of the body he saw in the famous Hangar 84. According to Balthaser, the body was humanoid. "About the size of a twelve-year-old child. They have the features of a human body except they have the larger eyes, bigger head. There's been descriptions of four fingers instead of five. Very thin. Not anything that anybody has ever seen."

E.T. PHONE HOME

BIG EYES? OVAL HEADS? Gray skin? That sounds like every alien we've ever seen in any bad science fiction movie. So did they pull their descriptions from the movies?

Not at all. This was 1947. The vast majority of movies about aliens visiting Earth hadn't even been conceived yet, much less produced and distributed.

The most famous of these movies, the original version of *The Day the Earth Stood Still*, didn't come out until 1951. For that matter, the 1940 science fiction story that that movie was based upon, "Farewell to the Master" by Harry Bates, didn't have a saucer, either. The craft in that story was described as ovoid, and hadn't flown to Earth, but just appeared here.

Take a look at the covers of the pulp science fiction magazines of the 1930s and 1940s . . . or lose yourself in some of Alex Raymond's truly great Flash Gordon comic strips. You'll be hard-pressed to find any saucers.

Sure, there are plenty of pointed rocket ships with fins and stubby wings—and more than a few giant spheres capable of traveling from world to world—but not many saucers.

So.

Which came first: the chicken, or the little green egg?

BEYOND THE QUESTIONS ABOUT ALIENS, whatever happened to the debris that was recovered from the Foster Ranch?

According to Dennis Balthaser, that debris was originally relocated to Wright-Patterson Air Force Base near Dayton, Ohio. But it didn't linger there long. "For reasons of better security," he explained, "the debris is probably at Area 51."

AREA 51

THE *OTHER* PLACE most closely associated with UFOs and extraterrestrials.

But where Roswell boasts an International UFO Museum and Research Center and attracts a constant stream of visitors and investigators, Area 51 is off-limits to . . . well, just about everyone.

Although it was first used as a military airfield in the 1940s—and it's been home to CIA spycraft as well as nuclear testing in the 1950s, Area 51 is so secret the government denied that it even existed until July 14, 2003.

There's only one road leading into it—a 13-mile-long dirt road that runs through some of the most desolate land you'll ever see. There's no cover, no place to hide, no way to approach quietly or secretly. There is no fence marking the boundaries of the base, only a gate with signs that promise you: USE OF DEADLY FORCE AUTHORIZED.

Dennis Balthaser believes that those signs are telling the absolute, deadly truth. In fact, he told us that we had no chance of getting into Area 51. At all.

So we did the next best thing: We found some people who had worked there. And we got them to speak to us.

Richard Mingus was a security guard at Area 51 in the late 1950s, and he remains both *proud* and *reticent* about his experience. To this day, he takes his security clearance quite

FACING PAGE, TOP
THE ROSWELL LOOK
Think about this: The standard image of the large-eyed, oval-headed, small-bodied alien only became popular after the Roswell incident.

FACING PAGE, BOTTOM
PRE-SAUCER CRAFTS
The "flying saucer" image didn't appear in popular culture until after the stories leaked out of Roswell. Before then, alien spacecraft were rocket-shaped or spherical.

seriously, and there's only so much that he'll say about his experiences at the top-secret base.

"I was told that what I was going to be guarding was more classified than the atomic bomb," he explained.

Did he have any idea exactly *what* was under his protection?

"We were told that it was a weather reconnaissance plane," he said, knowing that the government was probably lying to him. But Mingus wasn't upset. "That's the way it had to be."

So as much as I want him to tell us absolutely everything that he saw, Mingus is still honoring his orders. You have to respect him for that.

We asked him if he had access to the entire building. And Mingus admitted to us that he had peeked into one of the most restricted sites at Area 51, a hangar that was off-limits to all but half a dozen people.

"It was on a weekend," Mingus explained. "And I was walking, checking all the doors, making sure everything was secure. And I come up to this hangar that I'm not supposed to go in—and I crack the door. It's open."

So what did he see inside?

Mingus's response was immediate: "I've never told anybody."

So how else could Mingus help us?

"I don't like to get into an area that is very, very sensitive when you're talking about national security," he explained. "It's possible after I had gone that the program that Bob Lazar was assigned to would have been better off had they kept it as secret as possible, and a lot less people would know about it today."

There it was. Our next stop. Bob Lazar.

BOB LAZAR

WHEN YOU DEAL WITH BOB LAZAR, it's difficult to separate fact from fiction.

Lazar claims to be a physicist educated at MIT and CalTech, though neither school has records of his attendance. He claims to have invented a jet engine car capable of traveling more than 200 mph. He has a company that markets materials he asserts are based on futuristic technologies far beyond most contemporary abilities.

But by far his most notorious claim is that he worked in Sector 4 of Area 51 directly with alien spacecraft (which, of course, the government denies).

In his defense, Lazar says that the government disposed of all his records after he told the media in specific detail about the nine flying disc flights at Area 51. But here's where it gets even more interesting: Lazar didn't just claim to see alien saucers. He claims to have seen actual *aliens*.

To find the truth, we spoke with one of Bob Lazar's personal friends—and someone whose background could be far more trusted: John Lear.

Although quiet and unassuming, John Lear is quite simply one of the most accomplished pilots in U.S. history. He's flown 150 types of aircraft, he's the only pilot ever to earn every airman certificate issued by the FAA, he held 18 world flight-speed records, and he flew missions for the CIA. By the way, his dad, Bill Lear, invented something called the Learjet.

So when it comes to air travel, there are few people on Earth with more knowledge or experience than John Lear. So why is the government keeping its information about UFOs such a secret? Lear has a very simple answer.

"The aliens give us technology," Lear said. "And we use that technology."

I know. We were just as skeptical. Was this world-class pilot actually saying that the U.S. government was reverse-engineering alien technology for its own benefit?

"That's right," Lear said.

Did that mean his dad's company also reverse-engineered technology from the alien crash?

"Absolutely. Positively," Lear insisted. "As a matter of fact, the first company he had was Motorola, and then my dad formed his own company, became Lear Incorporated. He was very involved in all of this that was going on and went on to different projects."

OK. Time-out. That's one incredible claim. But. If what John Lear says is true, then we have an actual theory. Why would the government want to deny that aliens exist or that we've had contact?

Because the government itself is actually borrowing from alien technology.

Think about the historical context. In the years after World War II—and after Roswell—we were in a rapidly escalating Cold War, one that was being fought with espionage, scientific advances, futuristic weapons. At a time like that, you're going to tell me that we wouldn't do *anything we could* to maintain our technological edge over our enemies?

And before you decide, get this: In July 1947, something landed or crashed in Roswell, New Mexico, and was quickly gathered up and secreted away by the military.

Three months later, Chuck Yeager achieved something many scientists previously believed impossible: He pilots an aircraft through the sound barrier, doing about 771 mph.

Coincidence? Probably. But the postwar years *were* a time of astonishing technological advance. But now John Lear is claiming that his dad had contact with aliens and created his first mobile phone in the 1940s. This was before color television, wheels on suitcases, and in an age when doctors still believed cigarettes were good for you.

In fact, by 1969, Motorola had made a giant leap forward, as in: "one small step for man, one giant leap for mankind." Neil Armstrong phoned home using a Motorola, which just happened to work in space.

Officially, all the government will say about Area 51 is that it's an "operating location" near Groom Lake, Nevada. But we've confirmed that it's one of the leading sites for testing experimental aircraft and weapons and systems used by both the Air Force and the CIA.

Images of Area 51 never appear in U.S. government maps, or on aviation or navigation charts.

FLYING UFO AIRLINES?

There's only one road that leads to Area 51. So how does the government move its top-secret employees to and from the base?

You guessed it. Fly them.

The airline fleet includes six 737s that can carry up to 190 passengers each. Combined with five smaller jets, they can move up to 1,200 employees a day to a place that supposedly didn't exist.

Some say it even has a name: Janet Airlines.

Why Janet? Rumors say that the airline's name is actually an acronym standing for: Joint Air Network for Employee Transportation.

Now put yourself in the position of a conspiracy theorist and ask yourself this: What sort of facility would require an entire covert airline, with all that such an airline would need—pilots, maintenance crews, fuel, and everything else?

One that operates as far off the radar as possible—just the way a UFO research facility would be expected to.

To get to Area 51, you travel a road officially known as Route 375—but known to everyone else as the Extraterrestrial Highway.

Area 51 shares a border with the Yucca Flat region of the Nevada Test Site, where more than 700 nuclear tests occurred. Needless to say, it's not the best neighborhood.

At its center lies Groom Lake, the salt-flat remains of an ancient lake about three miles in diameter. To the south of the lake are a series of landing strips, a dormitory, a fire station, even such amenities as a baseball diamond and tennis courts. And, of course, there are surveillance cameras everywhere, always watching.

One of the most interesting things about the site is that it boasts more hangars than are typical for a military base—presumably to provide more cover against aerial surveillance.

But even more interesting than that is that Area 51 is built on top of an abandoned silver mine. That gives the place a whole network of underground tunnels and caves. Y'know what that means? You got it: The most sensitive and top-secret stuff may actually be *underground*.

PROJECT BLUE BOOK

SO BEYOND AREA 51, there's one other way to find out about UFOs. All you have to do is talk to eyewitnesses who have seen them. And y'know who's taken the lead on that front? The U.S. government. As former test pilot Allan Palmer told us, "In the Air Force, they had something called Project Blue Book—and every unidentified flying object and report that went in to the Air Force went in this project."

He's right about Project Blue Book.

Started in 1952 by the Air Force, the project was a way of determining whether UFOs posed a threat to national security. Before they were done, they examined 12,618 reported sightings.

Think on that a moment: 12,618 reported UFO sightings. According to the Air Force, 97 percent of the sightings were easily dismissed as natural phenomena—cloud formations, light effects in the sky—or man-made objects such as weather balloons. That still leaves 3 percent of the sightings as wholly unexplained—and perhaps inexplicable. That doesn't mean that there are alien spacecraft. But it also doesn't mean that there aren't.

Project Blue Book didn't make things much easier. Some insiders claim, in fact, that the percentage of unexplained phenomena may have been as high as 22 percent. That's a far cry from 3 percent—far enough that it makes you wonder about the honesty of the report altogether.

But here's the best part: When it came to changing minds in the military, guess whose mind got changed? One of the chief scientific consultants on the project, Dr. J. Allen Hynek.

Hynek joined the study as an avowed skeptic, but the amount of apathy and incompetence he encountered on the part of military investigators disgusted him to the point that he referred to Project Blue Book as going from the

BELOW
A SERIOUS
SCIENTIST
J. Allen Hynek (here identifying a supposed flying saucer as a chicken feeder in 1966) insisted that UFO research be approached rigorously.

J. Allen Hynek made an important contribution to the study of UFOs. In his 1972 book *The UFO Experience: A Scientific Inquiry,* Hynek introduced a three-step classification system for UFO sightings:

- Close Encounter of the First Kind: visual sighting of UFO

- Close Encounter of the Second Kind: visual sighting plus physical evidence

- Close Encounter of the Third Kind: visual sighting of UFO occupants or passengers

Sound familiar? That phrase "close encounter" quickly entered the vocabulary and gave its name to the Steven Spielberg movie.

Oh, and next time you see that movie, keep your eyes peeled toward the end, when the aliens are emerging from their spacecraft. You'll see one of the human observers step forward, a guy with a pipe and goatee. That's Hynek, finally seeing on a movie set what he always insisted we should search for in earnest in the real world: *evidence.*

investigation of the unexplained to the "explanation of the uninvestigated."

This is not to say that Hynek endorsed the explanation of UFOs as extraterrestrial spacecraft—only that he insisted that the phenomenon *still* hadn't been adequately investigated or explained. What he wanted, and continued to insist upon until his death in 1986, was the need to bring to bear the same level of scientific rigor on UFOs that we apply to biochemistry, gravitation, or any other field of scientific inquiry.

Today, Hynek is gone—and the rest of us are *still* waiting for that level of serious scientific investigation into the UFO phenomenon.

THE WHITE HOUSE

TODAY, our skies are filled with aircraft at virtually every hour of the day. To control and monitor that air traffic, we have the FAA.

Which brings us to John Callahan, who's decided to take a risk, defy an order, and tell his story.

Back in 1986, Callahan was the branch manager of the FAA's Tech Center in Atlantic City when a 747 came on the frequency, asking if there was any traffic in his area. The controller saw nothing anomalous on the scope, which was quickly reported to the 747 captain.

The pilot then reported seeing what he called "white and yellow strobe lights" at 11 or 12 o'clock— lights that indicated a craft *far* larger than an aircraft.

Larger than an aircraft? According to Callahan, the pilot was looking at this thinking, *"There's no airplane that big. It's like four times the size of an aircraft carrier.* He's flying a 747 that has an elevator in it. They have floors. It's like a two-story building flying in the air, and he's looking at something that is a massive, massive target out there, and he's assuming it's an airplane."

Did any passengers see it?

"All of the crew said the same thing," Callahan insisted. The crew even drew the same pictures of it. Yet according to Callahan, the unidentified aircraft that approached the 747 was so big, the radar picked it up as a *weather front.*

He described the craft as spherical and glowing. But the most astounding thing was the way it moved. The UFO zipped around so quickly that it appeared miles in front of the craft one moment and miles behind it the next.

Callahan reported the incident to his superiors, who immediately alerted the White House and summoned President Reagan's special investigative team. (Reagan himself claimed to have seen a UFO above Bakersfield in 1974—a bright white light that followed his airplane briefly, then disappeared straight up into the heavens.)

Returning to FAA headquarters after the 747 incident, Callahan found himself summoned to a meeting with an admiral who demanded a five-minute briefing on the UFO sighting. Upon hearing the details, the admiral canceled all of his appointments, cleared his schedule, and announced that the report would be taken directly to President Reagan and the president's scientific study team.

This was the moment—*finally*—a sighting that would get the attention and the investigative resources of the highest office in the land.

But when the scientific research team returned to visit Callahan, they were accompanied by three CIA officers.

Their message to Callahan was unmistakable: *This event never happened. We were never here. We're confiscating all data, and you're all sworn to secrecy.*

Knowing this was his only shot, Callahan asked one of the scientists what *he* thought the event was.

"Oh, it's a UFO," the scientist told Callahan. He glanced at the other scientists. "This is the first time they've ever had more than a few minutes of radar data to look at. . . . They're just drooling to get their hands on all this data."

What they did with the data and—more important—what it may have revealed about UFOs, we may never know. Callahan never heard another word about the incident that included the longest radar track of a UFO ever recorded.

Naturally, we asked him if he regretted not taking the story to the news media.

But to Callahan, it's a problem that can't be solved. "If you call the newspapers, the newspapers think you're a quirk because they've been brainwashed to believe that if UFOs existed, the government would know and the government would tell you."

And *that*, Callahan believes, is simply *not* going to happen. "They know what's good for you," he added chillingly, "and they know what you should be thinking."

IN THE END, our investigation into extraterrestrial life has led us from Roswell, to Area 51, to the White House.

ABOVE
PATHWAY TO THE UNKNOWN
Nevada Route 375 leads to Rachel, Nevada, and Area 51. Along the way, a spray-painted sign says, THE TRUTH IS OUT THERE. *Really.*

But before we could reach a conclusion, there was still one place left—the true final frontier. Outer space.

Which led us to Story Musgrave.

Musgrave is among the most experienced astronauts in history—a man who's left the earth six times. So did he ever see any alien beings when he was in orbit?

"Nope. But I *wanted* to," Musgrave admitted.

A trained scientist, he understands the inherent risks in looking for something you *want* to see. And he knows better than to let his wishes get in the way of what his scientist's eyes and experience show him.

But as he told us, "Every time you take a timed exposure with the Hubble, you get two thousand galaxies times a hundred billion stars. So within one picture you're looking at two hundred trillion stars. Aim the Hubble again and you have another hundred trillion stars." That many stars, at least some of which have planets, and at least some of which are theoretically capable of supporting life, and the possibility of intelligent extraterrestrial life is—

"Massive," Musgrave said. "It's a certainty."

More than that, he feels that there's little doubt that at least some of the species out there are traveling beyond their own star systems, particularly since many of these species are likely to be far older than us.

"They're doing interstellar travel," he said. "If you have an

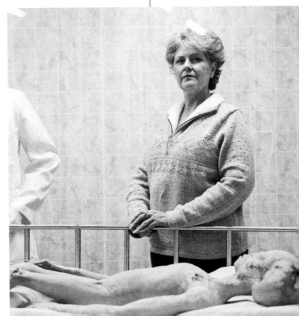

advanced evolutionary string [that] has been developing technology for a billion years, star travel *is* happening."

He likens the distance between us and the advanced extraterrestrials to the distance between his childhood and his first flight into space.

"When I was a kid, diesel locomotives [weren't] here. I was steam locomotive."

Indeed, in Musgrave's life, he went from "steam locomotives to space." Think of the human race going from an ox-operated drill press to the Internet. Now think what a billion years could accomplish.

It's a mind-boggling point. Today, there's more computing power in a cell phone than there was on Apollo 11, and that brought us to the moon and back. There are dozens of technological advances that every one of us has witnessed. So just try to imagine where we'll be in a hundred or a thousand years, much less the billion that Musgrave speaks of.

Of course, none of that definitively answers the question of whether or not aliens have visited us *here*. But that doesn't stop Musgrave.

"You have to look at the statistics. . . . It's statistical—it's the power of life. We have four million species here, not just a handful. Life has got the muscle and the ability to survive under a huge number of conditions. Add the massive time scale we're talking about and you have the possibility that life is everywhere."

Is he right? Time will tell, whether we like it or not.

CONCLUSION

THE MAJORITY OF STARS IN OUR UNIVERSE are more than one thousand light-years away, so that means it would take an alien spacecraft anywhere from a few years to more than a thousand just to get here, since nothing can travel faster than the speed of light. That's a mathematical fact—it's the universal speed limit—and physicists tell us that nothing can go faster than light.

But physicists also told us it was impossible to travel faster than the speed of sound—until Chuck Yeager proved them wrong in 1947 and broke the sound barrier. People thought it physically impossible for a human being to run a mile in under four minutes, until Roger Bannister did it in 1954.

Remember, just because something hasn't happened yet doesn't mean it's impossible.

I want to believe that we're not the only life out there. Ronald Reagan says he saw a UFO with his own eyes. So did Jimmy Carter. And Stephen Hawking, one of the greatest physicists of our time, thought it was a mathematical impossibility to say there's no other life. But listen to what Hawking said, because he also gives us a warning.

The great scientist reminded us that "we only have to look at ourselves to see how intelligent life might develop into something we wouldn't want to meet." He continued: "If aliens ever visit us, I think the outcome would be much as when Christopher Columbus first landed in America, which didn't turn out very well for the Native Americans."

So for as much as I want to believe, we need to always remember one thing: Be very careful what you wish for.

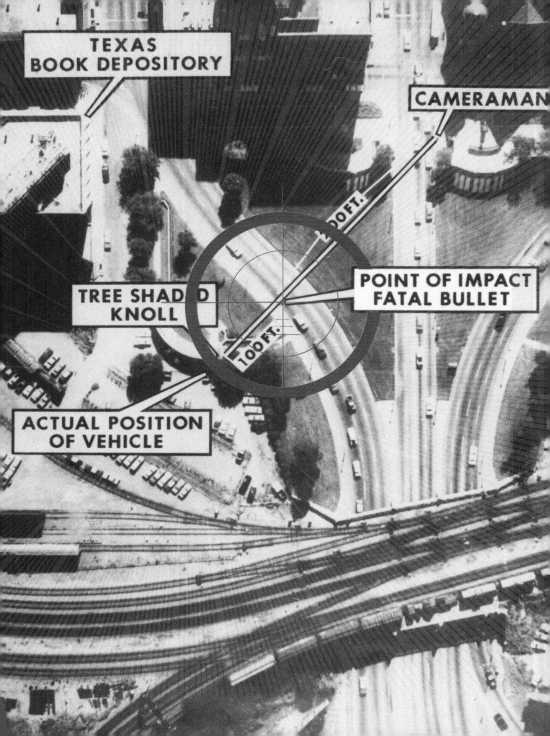

TEXAS BOOK DEPOSITORY

CAMERAMAN

TREE SHADED KNOLL

POINT OF IMPACT FATAL BULLET

ACTUAL POSITION OF VEHICLE

200 FT.

100 FT.

THE KENNEDY ASSASSINATION: THE TRUTH IS OUT THERE

LET'S BE VERY CLEAR. When you're counting down history's top conspiracies, there's only one that everyone agrees should be on the list. In fact, when it comes to decoding mysteries, the #1 request I get via email and Facebook messages is simply this: Tell us about the assassination of JFK.

So let me be even more clear: We can't do justice to the JFK assassination in a single chapter. Indeed, as we tried to lay it out, we realized it was so packed with craziness, it needed its very own top ten list.

So, without further ado, here are the top ten conspiracies within history's #1 conspiracy: the Kennedy assassination.

WHAT IF I TOLD YOU that no matter how much evidence there is that Lee Harvey Oswald acted alone, it'll never stop us from thinking that JFK's death was the result of a massive conspiracy?

It's amazing just how *many* conspiracy theories surround the assassination—though the number isn't surprising, especially when you consider that there's probably no single event in modern history that's been as relentlessly investigated. The investigations, in fact, may be the biggest part of the problem.

Put together all the official investigative commissions, reports, official reinvestigations, independent reviews of the evidence, journalistic inquiries, reenactments, documentaries, movies, literally thousands of books (fiction and nonfiction), not to mention countless off-the-wall and over-the-top websites, and you've got a situation that's a perfect breeding ground for confusion, differing interpretations, allegations, and refutations.

#10 OSWALD HIMSELF

ARRIVING AT LOVE FIELD IN DALLAS, President and Mrs. Kennedy left the plane and headed for a fence by the airfield, where a group of fans and supporters was waiting. For several minutes, the 46-year-old president and the First Lady shook hands, thanking them.

Someone handed the First Lady a bouquet of red roses, which she brought into the limousine. Texas governor John Connally and his wife were already sitting inside. The president and the First Lady sat behind them. And

BELOW
NOVEMBER 22, 1963
President John F. Kennedy and his wife, Jacqueline, arrived at Dallas's Love Field on a beautiful Friday morning. The roses were a gift from the crowd.

◇◇

"If somebody wants to shoot me from a window with a rifle, nobody can stop it, so why worry about it?"

— PRESIDENT JOHN F. KENNEDY,
THE MORNING OF HIS DEATH

◇◇

since the rain had stopped, the Secret Service didn't need the plastic protective bubble that could be put onto the car. Metal armor, bulletproof glass, and other countermeasures weren't even thought about until after this fateful day.

The trip to downtown Dallas was about ten miles. Not far at all.

As the motorcade arrived, crowds packed both sides of the street, waving flags and craning necks, eager to spot the young president and his beautiful wife, dressed in that stylish pink suit.

At 12:30 p.m., the presidential limo turned off Main Street at Dealey Plaza, making its way past the seven-story, redbrick building on the corner of Houston and Elm Streets: the Texas School Book Depository. It was going 11.25 mph.

Within six seconds, from the sixth-floor window, at least three shots rang out.

ABOVE
DEALEY PLAZA
The president's motorcade entered Dallas's Dealey Plaza at 12:30 p.m. CST. Within moments, the world would never look the same again.

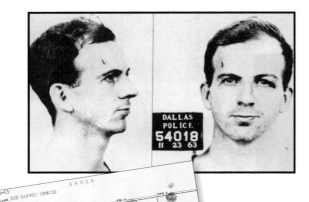

The president's hands moved to his neck. The bullet entered his neck to the right of his spine. The final shot struck JFK in his head, which exploded. The nation was changed forever.

THROUGHOUT THE COURSE OF HISTORY, there have been more than two dozen assassination attempts on the president of the United States. Four have been successful: Abraham Lincoln, James Garfield, William McKinley, and John F. Kennedy.

But only Kennedy's death took place in the age of modern communications as millions watched the events on nationwide TV. The networks almost immediately turned their attention to Dallas, coming on the air with live reports while there was still hope that the young president himself still lived.

Think about just that. Days after Lincoln was murdered, there was still a substantial portion of the population who thought that Lincoln was still alive. In the case of JFK, the whole world knew the moment the doctors pronounced him dead.

The only thing to compare it to would be the hours immediately following the terrorist attacks of

ABOVE
LEE HARVEY OSWALD
Lee Harvey Oswald was arrested and booked approximately 80 minutes after the assassination. That day, he left his money and wedding ring in the room where his wife was staying.

RIGHT
VIEW FROM BOOK DEPOSITORY

September 11, 2001. We all know where we were. We can recall it in a heartbeat. And like 9/11, as fast as the news swirled was as fast as the conspiracy theories began to proliferate.

It was the same in 1963. This was at the height of the Cold War. Suspicion turned toward the Soviet Union—or its puppet state Cuba. The military was put on alert. For all we knew, the United States was about to be attacked. Nuclear war seemed imminent.

Within 80 minutes of the assassination, an arrest had been made: Lee Harvey Oswald, a young 24-year-old high school dropout who worked at the book depository.

OSWALD HAD WORKED at the book depository for just a month, since mid-October. On the morning of the shooting, he was seen carrying a long, wrapped package, which he claimed contained "curtain rods." After the shooting, on the sixth floor of the book depository, three bullet casings were found on the ground, as well as a Mannlicher-Carcano rifle.

Less than two minutes after the shooting, police officer Marrion Baker ran into the depository and, with the building superintendent, ran upstairs. On the second-story landing,

ABOVE
TEXAS SCHOOL BOOK DEPOSITORY
Lee Harvey Oswald had worked at the depository for only a month. After the shooting, three shell casings were found on the sixth floor, along with a rifle.

BELOW
TRAGIC HEADLINES
At 2:02 p.m., Oswald arrived at Dallas Police Headquarters. At 2:38 p.m., Lyndon B. Johnson was sworn in as the 36th president of the United States.

DAILY NEWS 5¢
FINAL
KENNEDY ASSASSINATED
Johnson Sworn as President; Left-Wing Suspect Seized

The Dallas Morning News
KENNEDY SLAIN ON DALLAS STREET
JOHNSON BECOMES PRESIDENT
Suspected Sniper Nabbed by Police

Baker ordered a man who was 20 feet away to stop and walk toward him. It was Lee Harvey Oswald. But when building superintendent Roy Truly identified him as a fellow employee, Oswald was allowed to leave.

No question, Oswald matched the description of a "slender man, five foot ten" who aimed a rifle at the president from an upper window of the depository. That description was quickly transmitted to Dallas police, which is why 45 minutes after the shooting, police officer J. D. Tippit had words with a man matching that description. The man fired three shots across the hood of Tippit's police car, then came around back and fired a fourth shot into Tippit's head, killing him instantly.

Within an hour and 20 minutes after the assassination, and less than 30 minutes after Officer Tippit was killed, Oswald was seen at the Hardy Shoe Store, where store manager Johnny C. Brewer noticed him acting suspicious and nervous. Brewer followed him to a local Dallas movie theater, which — on this day, considering what happened — was itself a suspicious place to be. As Dallas police entered the theater, Lee Harvey Oswald pulled his revolver. But police prevented him from firing, taking Oswald into custody on suspicion of the murder of a police officer . . . and, many quickly assumed, the death of President John F. Kennedy.

At 2:02 p.m., Oswald arrived at Dallas police headquarters. At 2:38 p.m., Lyndon B. Johnson was sworn in as the 36th president of the United States.

By 3 p.m., the police were at Oswald's house. They asked Oswald's wife, who at the time was staying at a friend's house in Irving, Texas, if her husband owned a gun.

She said yes. But when she went to show the officers where it was, it was gone.

In addition, Oswald left his money—$170—on the dresser in the room where his wife was staying, along with his wedding ring. For some reason, on that day, he didn't want either of those on him.

Today, after shootings in schools and movie theaters, we've almost become accustomed to young twentysomething sociopaths who're delusional in their self-importance and need to prove their cause through violence. But as the details of Oswald's life were revealed, this didn't smell like another lone wolf.

First, he was a Marine sharpshooter. Second, back in 1959, after leaving the Marines, he moved to the Soviet Union and tried to renounce his U.S. citizenship (see Exhibit 1A, page 188, for a State Department telegram regarding his efforts). When the Soviets denied him citizenship, he attempted suicide. But he didn't return to the United States until

THE WEAPON

This was Oswald's Mannlicher-Carcano rifle (see photo below). The three shell casings found on the sixth floor of the book depository came from this gun. All bullet fragments from the victims and the presidential limousine were matched to the same rifle, as well as the bullet fragments found at the site of the attempted murder of General Edwin Walker (who Oswald had tried to kill on April 10, 1963).

The gun was ordered from a mail-order house in Chicago and shipped to someone named "A. Hidell" at P.O. Box 2915 in Dallas. (See Exhibit 1B, page 189.)

When he was arrested, Oswald was carrying a fake ID— a Selective Service card—with the name "Alek James Hidell" on it (Exhibit 1C, page 189). The documentation used to order the gun and to rent the P.O. box matched Oswald's handwriting. And the other person who was authorized to pick up mail at the P.O. box? Oswald's Russian-born wife, Marina. (Oh, and the name *Alek*? That's what Marina called Lee, since there was no equivalent of the name *Lee* in Russian.)

Yet to me, of all the gun evidence, the most damning is this: Oswald's palm print was found on the gun—on a part of the rifle that could only be touched when the gun wasn't assembled.

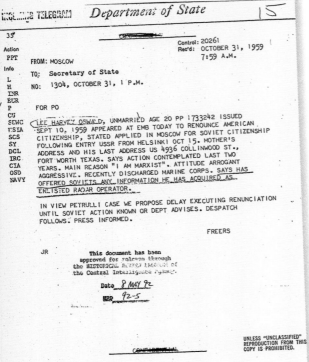

ABOVE
EXHIBIT 1A
*State Department
Telegram*

FACING PAGE
EXHIBITS 1B & 1C
*Gun receipt to A. Hidell
(top) and Selective
Service card for Alek
James Hidell (bottom)*

1961, which means he spent two years in the Soviet Union. Two years to meet people, make friends, and become part of America's greatest enemy. How could you not ask the question: Was he part of the KGB? A scripted assassin? Or even a CIA double agent?

It didn't help when, right after the shooting, as the press was shouting questions at Oswald and he was being taken from the jail elevator to the homicide and robbery office of police headquarters, Oswald replied, "I'm just a patsy."

And of course, there was the photo. In the court of public opinion, this famous *Life* cover article sealed Oswald's fate. He's not only holding a rifle and wearing a pistol, he's holding two Marxist newspapers—proof he could be working for someone else (which proves a conspiracy). Others said the picture was doctored (and c'mon . . . that proves a conspiracy *even more*). In fact, in Oliver Stone's *JFK*, a government agent *is shown* doctoring the photograph, and Jim Garrison is heard to say that the shadow on the face doesn't match the shadow on the body.

Yet more conspiracy, right? Except for the fact that government experts said that duplicating photographs causes barely perceptible changes that account for such differences — and concluded that no forgery was involved. Plus, when the full-frame photo was examined by the House Select Committee on Assassinations, it was determined to have been taken with Oswald's Imperial Reflex camera, to the exclusion of all other cameras. But c'mon — this is JFK — why trust the government?

How about the fact that Oswald sent a copy of the photo to his friend George de Mohrenschildt and wrote a message on it?

But handwriting can be faked, too, right? Then maybe it's worth listening to Oswald's wife, Marina, who repeatedly testified that she took the photographs at his request. But wait . . . she hated him, didn't she?

You starting to see the pattern? No matter how much proof you bring, there's always another argument to make. And in many ways — whether you see Oswald as master assassin or complete patsy — his biggest problem will always be this: He was murdered, too.

There would be no trial for Lee Harvey Oswald.

WHERE'S THE WINDOW?

Six years after Lee Harvey Oswald fired his famous shots from the sixth-floor window, General D. Harold Byrd, the wealthy Texas oilman who owned the book depository, made a slight modification to the building: He had the actual window removed, saying he didn't want vandals to steal it. Where'd he put it? This was Texas. He framed it and hung it in his mansion. Naturally.

But in 1970, another Southern eccentric, Aubrey Mayhew, bought the building. According to Mayhew, Byrd's handyman actually removed *the wrong window.* Mayhew says *he* has the right window (which, yes, he also removed). Where'd both windows eventually wind up? On eBay. Naturally.

Who's right? I don't even care. (FYI, Mayhew was right.) I just love that there are two Southern hotshots still fighting over it.

On Sunday morning, two days after JFK was killed, just after 10 a.m., Lee Harvey Oswald was set to be transferred from police headquarters to the county jail. Before the transfer, he was to receive a third interrogation, this time by the Secret Service, the FBI, and Captain John Will Fritz, head of Dallas's homicide section.

According to David W. Belin, who was counsel to the Warren Commission, "If no one else had joined the group, Oswald would have been transferred long before Jack Ruby ever got downtown. But at the last minute, Postal Inspector Harry D. Holmes—who had helped trace the money order Oswald used to purchase the rifle with which he killed President Kennedy—joined the group. Holmes's inclusion extended the interrogation by at least half an hour." In addition, Oswald requested to wear a sweater, which delayed the transfer as well.

As a result, that allowed enough time for a local night-club owner named Jack Ruby to arrive at the station. During the transfer, Ruby stepped from the crowd, shoved a revolver at Oswald's abdomen, and pulled the trigger.

Again, just reimagine the moment. You've got your hands on the most wanted man in America. Security should be tighter than anything the Dallas police had ever seen. And yet, a stranger steps out of nowhere—walks right past the cops—and guns down America's most wanted assassin. You think there were conspiracy theories following JFK's death? Now you've got a situation that seems almost *designed* to create an atmosphere of distrust, paranoia, and suspicion. Which is exactly what greeted the official government investigations.

#9 DUELING COMMISSIONS

SIX DAYS AFTER THE ASSASSINATION, President Lyndon Johnson, aware of the rumors and suspicions, authorized a commission to examine the tragic event. He appointed Supreme Court Chief Justice Earl Warren to head the committee, which quickly became known as the Warren Commission.

The blue-ribbon commission, made up of senators and congressmen from both major parties, as well as a former CIA director, spent ten months going through evidence, eyewitness accounts, and testimony from experts. They wanted to know:

- How many shooters were involved?

- Did the assassin(s) serve a larger goal than murdering the president?

- If so, was there a conspiracy behind the killing of JFK?

When completed, the commission's 888-page report reached a stark conclusion:

- Lee Harvey Oswald acted alone, firing the shots that killed President John F. Kennedy and wounding Texas governor John Connally. Oswald was not part of a larger conspiracy.

- Jack Ruby, who shot and killed Oswald in the Dallas police headquarters, also acted alone and was not part of any larger conspiracy.

ABOVE

JACK RUBY

Dallas nightclub owner Jack Ruby hung around with strippers and gamblers, but despite what you think, was never proved to have connections to organized crime.

With the release of the Warren Commission Report, the commission itself became the centerpiece of the rapidly multiplying conspiracy scenarios.

In 1976, the U.S. House of Representatives appointed a Select Committee on Assassinations (HSCA) to review the killing of President Kennedy, Martin Luther King, and the shooting of George Wallace. Their findings, released in 1979, were "that President John F. Kennedy was probably assassinated as a result of a conspiracy" and "a high probability [exists] that two gunmen were firing at the president."

Why the difference in outcome? The HSCA relied almost exclusively on an acoustical study (based on a recording presumed to have been made in Dealey Plaza), which was not examined by the Warren Commission.

Our own government couldn't decide what happened.

#8 JACK RUBY

HE'S THE ONE TO BLAME.

I mean it. If Jack Ruby hadn't killed Lee Harvey Oswald, we'd have our answers, wouldn't we? Or we'd at least get to ask the hard questions: "Who were you working with?" "What do you mean by *patsy*?" "Were you the only shooter?" Instead, thanks to Jack Ruby, thousands of new theories were born.

Most of them come from who Ruby was: the kind of penny-ante nightclub owner you've seen in dozens of cliché movies and novels. He hung around with strippers and gamblers, and was rumored to have connections to organized crime.

Yet even though he wasn't a deacon of the church, Ruby had a fierce patriotism and deep admiration for President and Mrs. Kennedy. So his motive? He didn't want the First Lady to have to come back to Dallas and go through the agony of Oswald's inevitable trial.

Good story. Makes sense. But y'know what else is a good story? A guy with underworld ties steps into the police station and, with a few pulls of the trigger, closes the final loose end for everyone. And it's even better when you think about this: How much did Ruby really admire Kennedy, considering he didn't even watch the parade? At the time, he was at the *Dallas Morning News* discussing his weekly ad in the paper.

In the end, it's tough to tell which version is true. But let's look at the actual moment: That Sunday morning, after taking care of some business at Western Union, Ruby went to police headquarters, where he was a known figure. People said hello, but no one stopped him or asked what he was doing. (Note that Ruby was at the Oswald midnight press conference that was held on Friday and could've shot Oswald then.)

According to prosecutor Vincent Bugliosi, whose *Reclaiming History* is the authoritative 1,600-page analysis of the assassination, had there been a line at the Western Union

DISTRUST FOR THE GOVERNMENT

How fast did conspiracy theories spread in the days before the Internet?

- Within days of JFK's assassination, more than half of people surveyed believed there was more than one shooter involved.

- After the Warren Commission Report was released, a whopping 87 percent believed there were multiple shooters.

- As recently as 2003, 75 percent of people polled believe that the Kennedy assassination was part of a conspiracy.

BELOW
RUBY SHOOTS OSWALD

office — or even one person ahead of Jack Ruby in line — the transfer of Oswald to the county jail would have been completed before Ruby was finished at the telegraph office. To Bugliosi, Mafia hit men don't take those kinds of chances . . . or cut things that close.

Timing is everything. And no one taught us that better than Jack Ruby.

On March 14, 1964, Ruby was found guilty and sentenced to death. Instead, he died in prison nearly three years later in 1967 (he didn't die right after his act, as many believe). The official cause of his death? "Pulmonary embolism."

#7 WHO ISN'T A SUSPECT?

WHEN ABRAHAM LINCOLN WAS SHOT, it was easy to know who wanted him dead. But in JFK's complex, interconnected world, the number of people who wanted him dead reads like a bad guy laundry list:

- The Soviet Union: Who better to kill our great leader than our greatest enemy?

- The Cubans and Castro: Right-wing Cubans were bitter over Kennedy's abandonment of the Bay of Pigs invasion and could've killed him for revenge; left-wing Cubans were loyal to the Soviet Union and could've acted at their behest. (And Oswald, not coincidentally, was a Cuba supporter. See Exhibit 1D.)

BELOW
EXHIBIT 1D
Lee Harvey Oswald's Cuba supporter card.

- Right-wing conservatives and Texas millionaires hated Kennedy's liberal stances on, among other things, race relations.

- The CIA and the military-industrial complex were enraged at Kennedy for his stance on Vietnam.

- The Mafia was supposedly livid about the Kennedy administration's ongoing investigations and prosecutions. The deaths of both Marilyn Monroe and Bobby Kennedy only added to this theory.

- And, of course, there are the Dallas police, the Secret Service, and LBJ himself, each theory with even more moving parts than the one before.

The point is, whoever the finger gets pointed at, it goes back to the one belief people can't shake: the idea that Lee Harvey Oswald couldn't have pulled it off alone.

#6 THE GRASSY KNOLL

ON THE DAY JFK WAS SHOT, the crowds in Dallas's Dealey Plaza heard the sound of gunshots. For five decades now, the questions remain: How many shots did they hear? And where exactly did that fourth shot come from?

The Warren Commission said three shots were fired, representing the three bullet casings found in the book depository. Then, in 1976, the House Select Committee on Assassinations (which had access to a sound recording that the Warren Commission didn't hear), concluded there was a "ninety-five percent chance or better that a noise as loud as a rifle shot was fired." They believe this to be the third of *four shots*—and that it didn't come from the book depository. So where did the fourth shot come from? An elevated piece of land known as the grassy knoll—to the right front of the passing presidential limo.

Why the change from the Warren Commission? According to Belin, the HSCA had originally *agreed with the Warren Commission,* deciding that Oswald *had* acted alone. Yet within a few weeks time, the committee flip-flopped. Belin said: "The committee's abrupt turnaround was caused by the mid-December testimony of two acoustic experts, Mark Weiss and Ernest Aschkenasy. They said they were ninety-five percent certain that the oscillating waves on a Dictabelt recording of police channel communications from the presidential motorcade indicated the presence of a second gunman firing a fourth shot from the grassy knoll."

But here's the problem. "Three years later, the acoustical-evidence testimony was refuted," Belin explained. Bugliosi agrees, pointing out that in 1982, "Twelve of the most prominent experts in ballistic acoustics in the country were commissioned by the National Research Council to reexamine the recording. The panel found 'conclusively' from other concurrent and identifiable background noise on the Dictabelt that the sound which the HSCA experts believed to be a fourth shot actually occurred 'about one minute after the assassination.'" That means that when the fourth shot was fired, the motorcade had already been told to go to Parkland Hospital.

Today, the findings of those acoustic tests don't matter. The damage has long ago been done. And that doesn't even include the trajectory of . . .

#5 THE MAGIC BULLET

ACCORDING TO THE WARREN COMMISSION, Governor John Connally was wounded by a bullet that first

FACING PAGE
AND NEXT PAGE
**KENNEDY'S
AUTOPSY**
At the request of the Kennedy family, photos and X-rays from the president's autopsy were withheld from the Warren Commission's investigation. It was a detail that would haunt the commission forever.

NAVMED N (Rev. 4-58) BACK

John Fitzgerald Kennedy

36. SUMMARY OF FACTS RELATING TO DEATH

President John Fitzgerald Kennedy, while riding in the motorcade in Dallas, Texas, on November 22, 1963, and at approximately 12:30 p.m., was struck in the head by an assassin's bullet and a second wound occurred in the posterior back at about the level of the third thoracic vertebra. The wound was shattering in type causing a fragmentation of the skull and evulsion of three particles of the skull at time of the impact, with resulting maceration of the right hemisphere of the brain. The President was rushed to Parkland Memorial Hospital, and was immediately under the care of a team of physicians at the hospital under the direction of a neurosurgeon, Kemp Clark. I arrived at the hospital approximately five minutes after the President and immediately went to the emergency room. It was evident that the wound was of such severity that it was bound to be fatal. Breathing was noted at the time of arrival at the hospital by several members of the Secret Service. Emergency measures were employed immediately including intravenous fluid and blood. The President was pronounced dead at 1:00 p.m. by Dr. Clark and was verified by me.

CERTIFICATE OF DEATH   COPY
NAVMED N (REV. 4-58) FRONT

1. SHIP OR STATION: The White House, Washington, D.C.

See NAVMED DEPT. for instructions regarding number of copies and submission.
IF UNIDENTIFIED INDICATE BY USING "X" AND CONSECUTIVE NUMBER HERE

1. NAME: President John Fitzgerald Kennedy

2. SEX: [X] MALE   [ ] FEMALE
3. RACE: [X] CAUCASIAN   [ ] NEGROID   [ ] OTHER (Specify)

4. STATUS: President of the United States
[ ] REGULAR ACTIVE   [ ] RESERVE ACTIVE   [ ] RETIRED   [ ] DEPENDENT   [ ] WIF   [X] OTHER (Specify)

5. LENGTH OF SERVICE (Years and months): 2 years 11 Months
6. AVIATION: [ ] YES [X]

7. FILE OR SERVICE: NA
8. RANK/RATE: NA
9. CORPS: NA
10. BRANCH OF SERVICE: NA

12. DATE OF BIRTH (Month, day and year): May 29, 1917
11. PLACE OF BIRTH (City and State or Country): Brookline, Massachusetts

15. COLOR OF EYES: Blue
16. COLOR OF HAIR: Auburn
13. AGE (Years, months) (Days, if under 1 year): 46 years 6 months
14. RELIGION: Catholic

20. MARKS AND SCARS (Based in health record): 4" scar 2nd, 3rd and 4th lumbar spine   4" scar upper left leg, well healed
17. COMPLEXION: Ruddy
18. HEIGHT: 72"
19. WEIGHT: 172

21. FINGERPRINT - STATE WHICH FINGER (Right index preferred)

31. DISPOSITION OF REMAINS: To the White House

32. DATE SIGNED: Nov

33. APPROVED COUNT
DATE SIGNED

23. NEXT OF KIN OR FRIEND (Relation, name and address): Mrs. John Fitzgerald Kennedy, The White House, Washington, D.C.

22. ADMITTED TO SICK LIST FROM (If on active duty, last duty station before current admission to sick list): The White House, Washington, D.C.
24. DATE ADMITTED TO SICK LIST (Month, day): November 22, 1963

25. PLACE OF DEATH: Parkland Memorial Hospital, Dallas, Texas
26. TIME OF DEATH (Month, day, year, hour): November 22, 1963 1:00p.m.

27.
CAUSE OF DEATH		APPROXIMATE INTERVAL BETWEEN ONSET AND DEATH
I. DISEASE OR CONDITION DIRECTLY LEADING TO DEATH. (This does not mean the mode of dying, e.g. heart failure, asthenia, etc. It means the disease, injury or complication which caused death.)	(a) Gunshot wound, skull	30 minutes
ANTECEDENT CAUSES. (Morbid conditions, if any, giving rise to above cause (a), stating the underlying cause last)	DUE TO (b)	
	DUE TO (c)	
II. OTHER SIGNIFICANT CONDITIONS. (Conditions contributing to death but not related to the disease or condition causing death.)		

28.
DO NOT WRITE IN THIS SPACE	1	2	3	4	5	6	7	8	9	10	11	12	13	14	15	16	17	18	19	20
	21	22	23	24	25	26	27	28	29	30	31	32	33	34	35	36	37	38	39	40
	41	42	43	44	45	46	47	48	49	50	51	52	53	54	55	56	57	58	59	60
	61	62	63	64	65	66	67	68	69	70	71	72	73	74	75	76	77	78	79	80

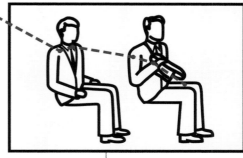

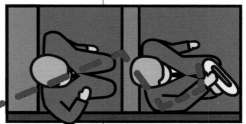

passed through Kennedy's back, exited from his neck, entered Connally below his armpit, exited below his nipple, wounded the governor's wrist, then came to rest in the governor's leg. That sounds like a *lot* of work for one bullet to do. Hence the term *magic bullet*—one that seems to violate the laws of physics and travel in a zigzag line.

To this day, many contend that the so-called magic bullet was in "pristine" condition. But that word *pristine* is used—over and over—by people who have never examined the bullet. In reality, the bullet is nearly flat on one side. It was found on a gurney believed to have been used to transport Governor Connally into the emergency room at Parkland.

For that reason, most people believe that one bullet couldn't do all that damage. But as Bugliosi argued, the bullet that struck Kennedy and then Connally was traveling *in a straight line,* just like bullets are supposed to. Connally was seated directly in front of the president, his body turned all the way to the right. As Bugliosi points out, because Connally had turned to face the president, the bullet could go nowhere else *but* into the Texas governor.

And by the way, just to be clear, Connally's entry wound was *ovoid,* meaning the bullet passed through *something else* before striking him. If it was a magic bullet—and didn't go through Kennedy—that wound would've looked quite different.

OK, then what about the fact that no other sharpshooter has ever been able to re-create Oswald's shots?

ABOVE
MAGIC BULLET
Many people believe a single bullet would have to have been "magic" to have traveled what they believe to be an impossible zigzagging trajectory, as shown above. But forensics say that's not the case.

#4 WHAT ABOUT THE FACT THAT NO OTHER SHARPSHOOTER HAS BEEN ABLE TO RE-CREATE OSWALD'S SHOTS?

THIS IS THE ONE TO PAY ATTENTION TO.

To match the shots from the book depository, Oswald would've had to have fired three accurate shots in six seconds with a bolt action rifle.

Sounds hard. In fact, an FBI marksman attempting to re-create the act required 2.25 seconds per shot, for a total of *6.75* seconds. That's one point for the conspiracy buffs. Oliver Stone's film *JFK* also reiterated that no one's been able to make the shot. That's two points for conspiracy buffs.

There's only one problem. It's not true. The Warren Commission's own marksman—Specialist Miller—fired three shots in as little as 4.6 seconds. Without a telescopic sight, the rate of fire was even faster. If that's not enough, here's the real kicker: A 1967 CBS reenactment gave the assignment to *11* marksmen. Their average time (without the telescopic sight) was 5.6 seconds.

Oswald was good. But so are others. Don't forget, Marines such as Oswald begin qualifying at 200 yards, then 300, then 500. That's *yards*. The shot for JFK was at a distance of a mere 59 yards for the back shot and

88 yards for the kill shot. And how good was Oswald? For rapid firing, he scored a 91 percent proficiency rate.

#3 THE ZAPRUDER FILM

IMAGINE A PRESIDENT BEING SHOT TODAY. Between cell phones and regular cameras, imagine how much footage we'd have of the event. But on November 22, 1963, the entirety of our footage comes from 31 photographers and, most memorably, the home movie of Abraham Zapruder.

The Zapruder film answers many questions even as it raises others. And one of the biggest: The film shows that the shooting and death of the president took *eight* seconds, not six, which means Oswald had even more time to make his shot.

Yet the film also shows the president's head appearing to snap *back* under the impact of the bullet—exactly the opposite reaction expected of someone shot from *behind*, as Kennedy was.

CLEAR SKIES— WHY DOES SOMEONE HAVE AN UMBRELLA?

It was a bright clear day in Dallas. So why was a man in the crowd holding an open umbrella as the president passed?

To some, the umbrella was a signal for the shooter(s).

The problem is, it wasn't. Though the umbrella—wielded by Louis Steven Witt—was a signal. It was Witt's signal that he felt Kennedy was as much an "appeaser" as the umbrella-toting Neville Chamberlain had been when Chamberlain attempted to make peace with Hitler before war broke out.

To this day, many say that the government is holding on to most of the JFK assassination records until all of the Kennedys are dead. "Not true," says Farris Rookstool III, an FBI analyst who was responsible for the custody of more than 500,000 pages of FBI classified records and is the only person to read the entire 500,000 pages on the assassination investigation. Rookstool was the one who transported the records from FBI headquarters to the National Archives and Records Administration Archives II in College Park, Maryland, where they reside today.

The best result from Stone's movie? The passage of the JFK Act of 1992, which declassified nearly 97 percent of the documents. As for the other 3 percent, the CIA's files were set for release in 2017. They are still being read.

BELOW

OLIVER STONE'S JFK *is responsible for an entire generation's understanding and misunderstanding of the facts surrounding the Kennedy assassination.*

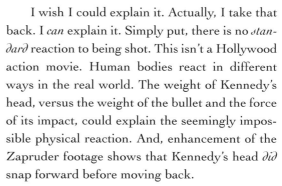

I wish I could explain it. Actually, I take that back. I *can* explain it. Simply put, there is no *standard* reaction to being shot. This isn't a Hollywood action movie. Human bodies react in different ways in the real world. The weight of Kennedy's head, versus the weight of the bullet and the force of its impact, could explain the seemingly impossible physical reaction. And, enhancement of the Zapruder footage shows that Kennedy's head *did* snap forward before moving back.

Yet despite the explanation, this is one of those details that just, well . . . it just smells fishy, adding to the lore of what really happened that November day.

#2 OLIVER STONE'S *JFK*

HERE'S THE MOTHER LODE. An entire generation's knowledge of the Kennedy assassination comes from one source: Oliver Stone's 1991 film *JFK*. Using real-life figures and New Orleans DA Jim Garrison as its hero, Stone seems to start with the truth. Garrison *did* try to refute the Warren Commission. From there, the film walks you through convincing conspiracies, cover-ups, misdirections, and governmental wrongdoings. In the context of the movie, it all seems so credible. But it bears almost no relation to the actual truth.

To list just a few of the claims made in the movie:

- Lee Harvey Oswald was completely innocent.

- There were six shots fired—and several shooters firing them.

- LBJ was in on it.

- A U.S. senator claims that no one has ever replicated Oswald's alleged shooting.

There's more, but you get the picture. And so did 20 million ticket buyers, not to mention tens of millions more who have seen the movie in subsequent years.

Indeed, Oliver Stone himself calls his movie a "counter-myth," created to rebut what he sees as the myths of the Warren Commission. And even Stone admits that much of his film is made up—fiction being used for dramatic effect. (The long scene where Garrison meets a high-level operative played by Donald Sutherland—who tells him everything that happened—was invented out of thin air. Kevin Bacon's character, a key witness in the film—who ties it all together—doesn't even exist in real life.)

To this day, when it comes to Oliver Stone's *JFK*, most people don't remember Stone saying he made up

◇◇◇

Is it any wonder that Vincent Bugliosi said that Oliver Stone's film "caused far more damage to the truth about the case than perhaps any single event other than Ruby's killing of Oswald"?

◇◇◇

In 1975, Belin was able to see the Kennedy photographs and X-rays himself, to answer questions about whether the CIA had been involved with the murder—and whether shots had come from the front as well as from the back of the president's limo.

"An independent panel of physicians helped to reevaluate all the evidence," Belin said. "The photographs and X-rays were horrifying, but they showed beyond a reasonable doubt that all the shots that struck Kennedy came from the rear."

Every medical panel—the independent panel in 1968 . . . the one in 1975 . . . the one in 1978—all agree. Yet the public barely knows these facts.

parts of it. They remember what they saw on screen. And even though the facts say otherwise, they prefer the version where this giant conspiracy somehow ties back to Lyndon B. Johnson, Kennedy's vice president.

Is it any wonder that Vincent Bugliosi said that Oliver Stone's film "caused far more damage to the truth about the case than perhaps any single event other than Ruby's killing of Oswald"? As for Bugliosi's own conclusion: "It would be hard to find any criminal defendant, anywhere, against whom there was as much evidence of guilt as there was against Oswald."

And yet . . .

#1 SECRECY AND COMPLEXITY

LOOKING AT THE FULL PICTURE, it's easy to point scolding fingers at so-called conspiracy theorists for keeping this story alive for so long. But the truth is, our society *needs* someone asking the hard questions. It keeps us honest and forces us to find truth.

Still, when it comes to the reasons why the facts surrounding the Kennedy assassination are such a mess, the very top causes of confusion come from these two areas:

- The secrecy the government shrouded this in.

- With hundreds of witnesses and thousands of exhibits, there's a natural complexity inherent in the case—especially one this traumatic.

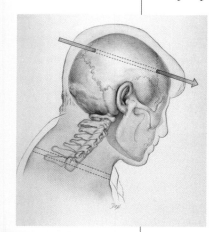

SECRECY:

As counsel to the Warren Commission, Belin said, "I believe that if there is a dominant reason why the Warren Commission Report has not been accepted by a majority of Americans, it is because all our investigative work was undertaken in secret."

Instead of open public hearings, the commission heard the evidence in private. As a result, the public didn't hear the key testimony of people like Howard Leslie Brennan, a 45-year-old steamfitter, who was staring right at the book depository—and whose testimony matched ballistics reports—and who reported seeing a man in the sixth-story window.

Brennan then turned to watch the approaching limo with JFK in it. "And after the president had passed my position, I really couldn't say how many feet or how far, a short distance I would say, I heard this crack that I positively thought was a backfire," Brennan testified.

"Then what did you observe or hear?" Belin asked.

"Well, then something, just right after this explosion, made me think that it was a firecracker being thrown from the Texas bookstore. And I glanced up. And this man that I saw previous was aiming for his last shot. . . . As I calculate a couple of seconds. He drew the gun back from the window as though he was drawing it back to his side and maybe paused for another second as though to assure himself that he hit his mark, and then he disappeared. . . ."

Brennan saw Oswald in that window. His report matched the ballistics. But the American people never heard the testimony.

This lack of evidence was only made worse by the Kennedy family, who convinced Chief Justice Earl Warren to make a truly unfortunate decision. As Belin described,

FACING PAGE
A SINGLE SHOT
This illustration accompanied the testimony of Dr. Michael Baden, a pathologist and chief medical examiner for New York City, before the House Select Committee on Assassinations in 1978.

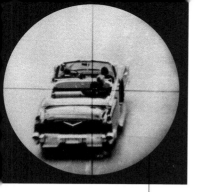

the Kennedys "persuaded the chief justice to with-hold the X-ray and autopsy photographs of President Kennedy from introduction into evidence as exhibits. Not only was the commission deprived of seeing these documents firsthand, but the public was denied an opportunity to have them independently examined by anyone seeking to verify the conclusions of the autopsy physicians who testified before the Warren Commission."

COMPLEXITY:

On top of that, the complexity of explaining the case was beat out by those rushing to explain it *first*. As Belin pointed out, one of the first big books that blamed multiple gunmen was based on this detail: that President Kennedy had said, "My God, I am hit" after the first shot.

According to the Warren Commission, the first bullet had come through President Kennedy's throat and then hit Governor Connally. But if the president had said those words *after* being hit, he couldn't have been wounded in the throat—meaning that the direction of the bullet was all wrong and there had to have been another bullet, presumably fired by another gunman.

So logical, right? Especially when you see that it was Secret Service agent Roy H. Kellerman, riding in the front of the limo, who said he heard what Kennedy said. But as Belin points out, "The author never told his readers what the other four passengers in the limousine remembered."

Secret Service agent William R. Greer, who was driving the limo, testified: "I never heard him say anything; never at any time did I hear him say anything."

Governor Connally said, "He never uttered a sound at all that I heard."

"It is virtually not assimilable to our reason that a small lonely man felled a giant in the midst of his limousines, his legions, his throng, and his security. If such a nonentity destroyed the leader of the most powerful nation on Earth, then a world of disproportion engulfs us, and we live in a universe that is absurd."

— NORMAN MAILER, *OSWALD'S TALE*

Mrs. Connally said, "He made no utterance, no cry."

Jackie Kennedy said, "I was looking this way, to the left, and heard these terrible noises. You know. And my husband never made any sound."

But rather than deal with the complexity of conflicting eyewitnesses (which is common in cases like this), the book planted one of the many seeds of doubt in the public consciousness. That seed—and so many more that came after it—are now a full-grown forest.

TODAY, NO MATTER THE EVIDENCE—no matter how many details point the finger at Oswald—the Kennedy assassination remains the one mystery that forever seems unsolvable. Why? Simply put: We just don't believe that Oswald did it all by himself.

Then how about this: We just don't *want* to believe that Oswald did it all by himself. We don't want to believe that the entire government can be jackknifed by a high school dropout. And even when we do, especially with our distrust of the government, all it takes is one piece of evidence to put us back on our skeptical paths.

BUT WHAT ABOUT . . . ?

THE MAN IN THE DOORWAY

One curiosity that seems to never go away is an AP picture, taken at the time of the shooting, showing a slender, dark-haired man standing in the doorway of the book depository. Some say it's a picture of Oswald. If that's accurate, obviously, there's no way he killed Kennedy.

Case closed, right? Well, not really— considering that the man looks incredibly like Billy Lovelady, a fellow employee at the book depository, even down to the shirt that Lovelady wore that day.

THE BABUSHKA LADY

Here's another one. In one frame of the Zapruder film, at the exact moment the presidential limousine passes and the shots ring out, you can see a woman standing on the curb of the street. The woman, identified by conspiracy buffs as the Babushka Lady, is holding something in front of her eyes. Some say it was a camera.

If it *were* a camera— based on her angle and how close she was—she'd have a far better image of the actual kill shot.

So what happened to the woman? She's never come forth. Some say she disappeared. Or maybe she's not holding a camera, skeptics argue.

In 1970, a woman named Beverly Oliver claimed to be her. The problem? Her story didn't hold up for a number of reasons. One, she named the wrong kind of camera used (it didn't

exist in 1963). Two, she claimed that agents seized her film (which is what many believe to this day), but don't forget this: She also recanted that story on at least one occasion.

THE SECRET SERVICE PROTOCOLS

On the day of the shooting, many point to the fact that the Secret Service didn't keep to their own safety protocols, as if to suggest that they did a bad job on purpose. Let me be clear: I don't believe that. But I do believe in human error—especially when you're trying to do a security sweep on one of the largest cities in America. To that

point, when the House Select Committee on Assassinations looked at it, they concluded:

> "In 1963, Secret Service regulations governing escort security for presidential motorcades provided that buildings along the motorcade route had to be inspected whenever the motorcade route was a standard one that had been used in the past. President Kennedy's Dallas motorcade route had been the standard route for motorcades for years; President Franklin D. Roosevelt, for example, had visited Dallas in 1936 and traversed the same route in a motorcade (although in the opposite direction). Nevertheless, on November 22, 1963, when President Kennedy visited Dallas, the Secret Service's own guidelines were violated, and no inspection of the buildings along the motorcade route was made."

And want more proof of human error? The House got it wrong, too. Farris Rookstool III, a former FBI analyst who served as the bureau's expert on the JFK assassination and additionally served on the FBI JFK Task Force, told us, "Roosevelt and Kennedy's parade routes were not identical. They were similar. Roosevelt traveled by train and departed Union Station north on Houston Street and east on Main (traveling in the opposite direction of Kennedy's parade route). FDR then used Commerce Street to return for his luncheon. Ironically, USSS Dallas Field Division SAIC Forrest Sorrels worked both Roosevelt's visit and JFK's."

MYSTERIOUS DEATHS

It's one of the most persistent theories out there: that dozens of different witnesses connected to Oswald and Jack Ruby suddenly started dying mysteriously, as if some specialized hit squad was murdering them one by one.

Many point to the death of Dorothy Kilgallen, who claimed to have interviewed Jack Ruby, and who was later found dead. Others point to the death of Marilyn Magyar, who worked as an exotic dancer in Ruby's Carousel Club — or to Karen Bennett Carlin, one of the last people to speak with Ruby.

Yet when you look at the individual deaths, Kilgallen didn't die until 1965, Magyar was killed by her husband in a domestic dispute, and Carlin wasn't even dead at all (she actually didn't die until 2010).

Are there some deaths that are harder to explain? Sure. But this is hardly the work of a hit squad that fanned out days after the 1963 shooting. According to Rookstool, "The notion that there was a 'clean-up hit squad' to go around the country eliminating 'people who knew too much' has always been one of the most humorous notions. I have never encountered anyone who 'knew too much.' Most I know simply don't know enough. Which, yes, is a subset of heart disease, which is the number one killer of the general population.

DISTANCE TO STATION C	181.9 FT.
DISTANCE TO RIFLE IN WINDOW	218.0 FT.
ANGLE TO RIFLE IN WINDOW	18°03'
DISTANCE TO OVERPASS	307.1 FT.
ANGLE TO OVERPASS	+0°44'

ABOVE TOP
THE FATAL MOMENT
A still from the Zapruder film, the most famous home movie in history.

ABOVE MIDDLE & BOTTOM
ATTEMPTS TO UNDERSTAND
Statistics and a limousine photo from a reenactment that was conducted to make sense of the crime.

Listen to what Robert F. Kennedy Jr., whose own father was assassinated, said in January 2013: "The evidence at this point I think is very, very convincing that it was not a lone gunman. . . ." Kennedy Jr. doesn't say what his evidence is. But he does admit that his own dad, who as attorney general had been relentlessly going after the Mafia, felt that his actions might have caused the Mob to have the president assassinated.

Hard to shake, right? But for me, the most telling part of who killed JFK is simply this: Our history reveals our own biases.

- In the 1960s, we blamed the Soviets, the Cubans, and, of course, the Establishment: right-wing conservatives and Texas millionaires.

- In the 1970s, with Vietnam and Watergate, it was the CIA who killed him.

- In the 1980s, as the *Godfather* movies led to *Scarface,* it was the Mafia.

Decade after decade, the enemy we search for is always a reflection of our deepest fears—a perfect reflection of us. We are the Ahabs; JFK is our stunning white whale. And the harder we search, the more we reveal our own insecurities. Our own fears. Our own weakness. Never forget, the greatest battle we'll ever face is the battle within ourselves.

To this day, it is perhaps the true legacy of JFK: The president who showed us the highest of our expectations also revealed the depth of our anxieties.

In the end, to me, this is what our show *Decoded* was all about: Not just counting down the top conspiracies through history—but reminding us exactly *why* these stories carve at our core—and what they say about us as people.

ACKNOWLEDGMENTS

THIS BOOK (like the TV show) wouldn't exist without the hard work of so many people. So massive thank-yous to the following: First, my wife, Cori, who believes *with* me. My sister, Bari, who loves when the story gets scary. And in honor of my Mom and Dad, a special thanks for letting me watch *All the President's Men* all those years ago. My agents on this, Jill Kneerim and Rob Weisbach, for cheering from the very first chapter. And to Rob, who is the real reason the HISTORY network found me. Hope Denekamp, Caroline Zimmerman, and all our friends at the Kneerim, Williams & Bloome Agency.

Needless to say, I couldn't do this without the rest of my family: Bobby, Dale, Ami, Matt, Adam, Gilda, and Will. Or without Noah Kuttler. He's the best believer of all. And the one who sends me the most obscure details in here. Also to Chris Weiss and Judd Winick, who still make fun of me the same way they did when we were eighteen.

None of this would have been possible without our family on the *Decoded* television series and at the HISTORY network, starting with Nancy Dubuc, who was our fearless leader from the very start. David McKillop helped bring us life, and Dirk Hoogstra kept us there. I admire them both so much. I also need to single out Russ McCarroll for steering every single episode we did. His impact cannot be overstated. I'm honored I get to work with him, but even more honored to count him as a friend. Special thanks also to Susan Ievoli, Kristen Burns, and every single person at HISTORY who built this dream with their own hard work.

THE CONSPIRACIES TEAM

BUDDY LEVY is the author of the narrative histories *Geronimo, River of Darkness,* and *Conquistador.* His website is buddylevy.com.

CHRISTINE MCKINLEY is a mechanical engineer and author of *Physics for Rock Stars,* a book about how physics can be used to create a more glamorous and exciting life. She now has an arrest record thanks to her work as an investigator on *Brad Meltzer's Decoded.*

SCOTT ROLLE is the former States Attorney for Frederick County, Maryland. He is a graduate of the FBI National Law Institute, and a major in the U.S. Army Reserve. He lives in Frederick with his wife, Stacy, and their four children.

Tina Gazzarro is my true sister and this show would be lost without her. We're also so lucky to have Gary and Julie Auerbach, Gail Berman, Lloyd Braun, Jared Heinke, and the rest of the dream teams at Go Go Luckey and Berman/Braun. And to be extra clear, the work of Ron Brody, Charlie Cook, Bill Langworthy, Mark Cole, Bryn Freedman, and the rest of our incredible crew is what made it all come together. They are the true lifeblood of the show. Without production, there is no production.

Of course, without Buddy Levy, Christine McKinley, and Scott Rolle, I'd just be a guy in front of a green screen. They do the hard work and deserve the real credit. Let me say this clearly too: I feel honored to be part of *their* team.

Special thanks also to Joseph LaPolla, who brought me here; our Florida team at Sterling Studios: Roy Liemer, David Fruitman, June Czarnecky, Roger Prehoda, Robin Ryant, and Lori Smith; all the incredible experts and authorities who gave their time and brains to every episode; and, of course, my family and friends, who always stand with me.

Additional thanks to Farris Rookstool III, who lent us his incredible expertise on the Kennedy assassination and helped keep me honest about all the facts in there. Farris, you're truly one of the best. Thanks also to Archivist of the United States David S. Ferriero, plus Matt Fulgham, Miriam Kleiman, Trevor Plante, and all our friends at the National Archives. Want more amazing details about history? Go visit them.

Finally, let me thank the generous and amazing Keith Ferrell, my cowriter and voice within these pages. Plus Chris DeRose for his help with the JFK research.

I also want to thank everyone at Workman Publishing: Peter Workman has passed away, but this all now exists in his honor. Huge appreciation also to Suzie Bolotin, Walter Weintz, Page Edmunds, Claire McKean, Doug Wolff, Carol White, Barbara Peragine, Jarrod Dyer, Jessica Wiener, Selina Meere, Courtney Greenhalgh, and Justin Krasner. A massive thank-you must go to Lisa Hollander, for doing such beautiful design work. An extra thank-you goes to Bruce Tracy, the only editor crazy enough to try and take on a book with this many moving parts. And of course, I want to thank my friend Bob Miller, for leading us all on this endeavor. Thank you, Bob, for your never-ending faith.

CREDITS